The Poetic Ramblings of a Disenchanted Child

Danny Warren

Printed in the United States of America.

Library of Congress Control Number: 2022947714

ISBN   Paperback   978-1-68536-879-1
      Hardback   978-1-68536-880-7
      eBook   978-1-68536-881-4

Westwood Books Publishing LLC
Atlanta Financial Center
3343 Peachtree Rd NE Ste 145-725
Atlanta, GA 30326

www.westwoodbookspublishing.com

HEREWITH:

Is a collection of poems, perhaps a little jaundiced of vision, perhaps not, depending on the abiding perceptions of the reader, but in the overall context, a singularly mild attempt at humorous levity: This little collection embraces the personal inclinations and the personal experiences that relate to this writers own life: It remains an expression of all of the home truths that have littered his wayward life with promises so that they finally surrendered, in the end, all true purpose and providing in the end a survival ethos that remains just that little bit less amenable.

Poetry has always been the tool of his expression: It has provided the subjective facility of truth and tact, while also enabling the writer, hopefully, to unburden the soul of otherwise unrequited frustrations: It is his sincere hope that this outpouring of random signals and messages might serve as an emotional palliative for all of the hopes and all of the ambitions that have so addled the sorry lives of readers whose needs were not really that different from those of the writer, at the end of the day

The overall intention of this collection of poems is to provide comfort and pleasure: They are comprised, randomly of sonnets, poems that rhymes, and many indeed, that do not: There is even the occasional one that has been written in an acrostic style.

My interests include aviation, science subjects and a rash of political interests of which I am not rigorously involved, except when it is with my wife: I am aged 75; I have tried to lead a generous and honest life, littered with the best of intentions; some successful; some not so much, but all eventually mitigated by events that have interrupted these episodes, in this so active time line, that I have not always been able to properly control, to my total satisfaction.

So dear reader! Do take your time in deciding if this kind of effort is the one that you really wish to embrace: If you do perhaps decide to give it your unqualified attention, may it perhaps give you as much pleasure as it has given to me.

CONTENTS

A Last Sleep

Darkness is the comforter of the coward
In his desperate pursuit of one more lie:
Gateways to helplessness
Yawn their invitation
To destitution and regret
In the tranquil balm
That is nocturnal oblivion:
Yet still I wait in expectation,
Real or unreal
For a word that will finally allow transcendence
To this waif trapped in the miseries
Of illusion and imperfection:
Smiles and light are so life
In the longing that is existence,
Littered with rewards gloomily greeted,
As if everyday gifts were a monotony
In survival's necessary requirement
For the function of an endless sleep.
Waking dormant permanence
Is the legacy of this impromptu eternity
Where time will always be a liar
In this interlink of lives
And promising absolution:
Once more must I awaken,
to smile at a song,
Struggling to recall the relevance of words
Whose importance whispers throughout the wastage
That is countless tempting dreams,
To a sleep that will finally last!

Aftermath

I bare my pain
And languish in my misery and loss:
Your flowers are my flowers
In the perpetual severance
Of all of our memories and joys:
Darkness envelopes my consciousness,
Blanking out all sensation,
Save the need to hold you:
Tears weave a tenuous deliberation
Of wanton melancholy,
Carving a path etched by repetition-
Wasting, dejected eyes:
All I can give you is my silence
And my outstretched heart:
Let it sustain you
Until we are together again.

Age-Old Age

Rusting rhythms sing their sad song
In a world of newer dreams,
Dedicated to the last stone
Thrown into a ringing stream.

Memories of ancient places,
Symphonies of stranger times;
All recorded as the smiles
Of expectations other rhymes.

Dangerous and optimistic;
Hopes in plenty show the way:
Age with all its mild progressions,
Keep the world of death at bay.

Distances are but a whisper,
Little left to want or need:
Lifetime saved and lifetime ended;
Aged insensitivity.

Airship

Silence hums in a drifting void
Breath'd by hints of air,
Borne on the gasp of a timeless memory;
Serene in its solitude:
Led like some fortunate mariner
Through mountainous billows of grace and form.
Cloud worlds mould and praise the sky,
Stately, delicate,
Proclaiming their grandeur.
We are together in a companionship
Of mutual contemplation,
Feeling oh so gently
As though the caress of a touch might yet alarm
This alien eye:
Blessed calmness assails the senses,
Pleading with me for the familiar perception
Of an oh! So tainted Earth:
Solidity, with its transient reluctance,
Parts for an embrace and a welcome:
The delicacy of gossamer
Greets me with its absorption;
The final caress that is absolution:
I used to think I knew you,
World of worlds;
Intensity becalmed with a sweetness
That is final restitution:
Now all I can do is to gaze at you
In grateful wonder;
For all the world like a God,
At the magnificence of it all.

Altar Boys

Incense sweating,
Altar dressing.
Brassy, pompous,
Sacred homage.
All I have is supplication,
Morning mass or benediction:
Upright standards in precision,
Three a side in fair division:
Recall that rare moment when
I casme in prayer to greet again
Your tabernacled sentinels;
Understanding, unashamed.

Hello, Goodbye

Where are you staying, my darling?
You're not in the same place as me!
I see in your distant reflections,
The glaze of your long history.

I so want a share of your silence,
To know if you're lost or in pain:
To see if the being that lives in yourself
Is part of a different refrain.

And how long ago was it darling,
You seemed not to recognise me?
It seems such a long time ago now,
You acted irrationally.

How much do I weep at your action's;
You're so unaware of my pain:
You just don't know how and you just don't know why,
Still, you do it again and again.

I'm so sad, I know it's all over;
You don't see my face anymore.
The dreadful affliction that Alzheimer named
Has finally closed your mind's door.

And yet in your quiet situation,
You still hold the key to my heart:
Perhaps in your strange distant new netherworld,
You still know that we'll never part.

Ambition

Again, you greet me,
Awakening as a somnolent flower;
Disgorging optimism
And radical expectation:
One more new day!

Motivation, stimulus and greed
Demand the best
That I can give,
That I still make my way,
Come desperation.

Vague memorials:
Pathways etched in stone,
Of failures past and gone,
Will be the guide
That steers me ever onward
To journey's end.

Dear Angel

I never ever met you, or perhaps I did
In a long-ago sleep.
You inspired all of my painful longings,
Fading with the abruptness of an unfinished whisper
In another desiccated dawn;
Investing a linger like the ache of some lost perception,
An unsustainable memory that leaves only pain
And melancholy to remember you by.
I tell myself that we'll meet again one day
In another time that will transpose itself into a new dream state,
And instants of real disappointment
Are merely the foretaste of a better tomorrow,
And you will be my reality forever:
Am I permitted the time to enjoy these confusions,
And the selection of these moments;
Time that I might finally be able to enjoy them in:
These presences and pleasures are as real to me
As the sweet scent that time strews
Throughout the essence that is my imagination
And my existence?
My best measures are in the care that is part of me,
With me,
Watching me,
Being the very best that I can be;
Ever present in this waking dream.

9/11 Swansong

Betrayed by wretchedness and bated breath
Do throes of end day founder in farewells,
At all the misery impressed beneath
This ruined heart wherein misfortune dwells.

And tears and fortitude plead for remorse,
At lost and found objection to a time
So carelessly commanded and endorsed
As real achievement in this world of crime.

Then whisper loud your venture with appeal,
And shout, but secretly your devil's name:
That all who need this sorcery might kneel
In meek subjection to this day of shame.

What greatness lies in wishing for some part
Of one last chance to heal this broken heart?

Gardener at Arromanche

Expansive disparate symmetry
Fawns at the day with familiar pains;
A swathe of tears upon this shroud of death,
Meadow of ephemeral hospitality:
Quiet submissions defy the whispers
That utter wherever stones
Share the gentle breaths,
The briefest murmurs
That are all of those sad exchanges;
Lost tales and latent memories:
And what is it that you hear
With your own sad basket of recollections,
As you ply your solitary dedication
Throughout these desolated rows of indignant waste,
Preening and combing
Secrets and stories
That they, at the very least deserve to have saved
From the mishaps of their own abbreviated existences?
Pause at a name,
A time, a memory
You once knew
Of the histories
That are all of the souls,
In this unhappy place.

Artistic Fix

Joy of liberty
Tempts fear and pain,
Expressions of a heart:
Eager sustenance for a pen
Weighted down with deliverance:
If truth hangs heavy
With the doubts and hesitations
Of a less than happy spirit,
How much more difficult will it be
When sad conviction
Only offers the certainty
That an open heart
Retain the curiosity
Of its own dilemma?
Personal structure is experience;
A pain shared,
Only serving to enhance
The misery that is sad recollection
In others,
With their rekindled memories,
Best forgotten:
True poetry must be truthful
Or it will fail in the mire
Of its own hypocrisy:
Artistic persistence,
Even at the risk of misunderstanding,
Is important if there is something to say;
So say it well,
That truth might win the day!

Bad

It's probably the first word that I ever learned;
I was required to understand the meaning of:
How soon should I begin to really know a sin,
Equating it to every action ever done,

Or saw, or thought, or badly enough wanted
That might be vaguely construed as unclean
By my controllers, often self-appointed,
With disconcerting, barely concealed glee?

"TOO BAD!" became in very shortened order,
The purpose of life's stipulation stone:
Bad boys, bad girls, bad food, bad simply everything
You never, ever want to bring home

To Mummy and to Daddy for inspection,
And comforting smiles, surreptitious glows
Of condescending, righteous approval:
The sort of good thing every parent knows.

Yet bad has become pretty rife with day and age,
With bigger better bad things all the rage:
It's even become hipper to become badder
Than all the badder people up the stage.

Yeah! 'Bad' is good now like a false affliction:
A readiness for comfort and a plea,
To all that childhood threatening and posturing;
To just leave me alone and let me be.

Bankrupt

Laughter lies like a bedraggled swansong,
In eyes where faith is glazed by new-found fears:
Unsaid admissions, shattered like a penance;
Or so it seems for unremembered years.

In darkness, comfort dwells, a gentle thief;
Conditioned subterfuge of septic charm,
For doubtful mind to drift and dwell beneath;
Deceptive absolution, freed from harm.

Yet still, harsh realisms pray and bloom
Its whispers of insidious intent,
And mischief moments cultivate the fading gloom
Of misery and sorrow and regret.

Ah! Folly of possession let me be,
A saving grace, spirituality.

Maldon Barge Race

Forested castles, stately, serene,
Dowager passaged, voluptuous beamed:
Glorious, grandiose, breathless of air,
Tranquil, mysterious, devil may care.

Signalling readiness, billowed, uncurled,
Pupescent chrysalis, image unfurled:
Watching as they saunter languidly by;
Waiting crowds cheer as the gull's swoop and cry.

Carnival-spirited sunshine and smiles,
Sun-stroked pedestrians seeking for miles
Stroll on the promenade, gazing away:
Mastheads receding, a glorious day.

Emptiness, misery, now that they're gone:
Fine upright megaliths sailing for fun:
Will we see them again, know where they've been?
Never a race this one, more of a scene.

Dear Ben

Month's pass,
Deceptive lies
That promised a better tomorrow,
Tempered with time:
Betrayal still feeds
On that last long look
Of eyes that so wanted to believe
That everything was still the same
In the end;
Desertion denies understanding:
Total loyalty and trust,
Squandered in the end
With a betrayal that has no bearing
Or comprehension for you:
A moment that was entrusted
To me to cherish
In a more tremulous time:
Home was always endless greetings,
Flavoured with your own account
And your undiluted affection:
Live on in me.

Bestsellers

Number one bestsellers seem like two-a-penny dreadful's;
Buy it if you dare, there will be others right behind:
Take your time in choosing it if you have time to spare
To see if rhyme or reason lurk within the lines.

Languish in the misdemeanour of some sordid theme
Laced with relish on the platter of a dream:
Find your life reflected in the image, in the strands
Gently filtering through mystic super schemes.

Live the expectations of the packaging and print
And the promise of some scrumptious delight,
Cast in stone and offered as the prelude to the feast,
Cased within each tasteful page in black and white.

Disinter a heartbeat as the multi folded slights
Of a thousand helpless moments are proposed,
Naked and forever in this tale of cryptic blame
With the reader and the writer juxtaposed.

Birth, Unbirthed

I am the endless alchemy of breathless need,
Entreating you with nervousness and hungry greed:
Predacious expectations mouthed with mindless glee,
Beg absolution for the very best you give to me.

Birthday breasted, bare indulgences repast;
Serve all illusions of existence, meant to last
Into eternity for goodness sake and goodness past,
And who will have it otherwise when dies are cast.

Until brave adolescence teaches greater sins,
And thankless retribution is survivals,
Decision times are not the comforter that hymns
Proclaim as goodness in a world where evil wins.

For truth is always casualty when might or slight,
Sees envy and intolerance as black and white:
In worldly ways, compassion's needs are often right
When naive expectations lead you to the light.

Birthday Boy

I look through watered eyes to watered eyes:
Tears are pleasures prize, tears of surprise
Wallow in my nakedness and my despair,
In closeness and in warmth against this dreadful air.

Are longing and desire the only friends I feel;
Terrified, awaking chitter chatter pleas?
Hands that hardly hug, embrace this fear so near,
Grasping tender eyes that see so deep, so clear.

Black and White

Have I appeased your monochrome insistence;
Absorbed your philanthropic masquerade
Of flaccid gratitude and stilted promises,
Consistent with your normal days to days?

Your regulation orders without question,
Impressed in habit of the starkest form,
Perverted liberties and imperfections;
A stultifying mirage of the norm?

So have I suffered from your stark precisions,
Expressed as dogma, sharp as black and white
And read all over, prayerful intermissions
Of faith inlaid with shame and guilt and fright.

This image in my mind is plain to see,
As smiles and sadness visit equally.

Blind Estate

Comforted in glazed seclusion,
Light lays its warmth
To his unrelenting measure:
Visionary chords are life
In the tepid stall that is tactile memory:
Air wafts in and out of idled lips;
Rhythmic reminder of the weakness
That constitutes continuation;
The hush that is all of his existence:
Audio-visual diversion,
Cursing the pain that is repetition;
Fading into a more relevant reverie:
Dark silence hangs like a pall
In this void of colourless obscurity:
Tentative hands extend,
Seeking for recognition of an object
Placed the among other
Comfortable familiars:
Sightless resignation;
The sink of opaque secrets,
Intent on a prefabricated world,
Made favourite with time.

Book

Do I still smell good to you?
Fingers lovingly caressing;
Delighting in your pleasure truths:
You are my resurrection and my life;
Dear divinity, clouded by illusion
And misconception:
My prayer is my plea
And my word is my being
And my existence.
Life is in me
And this world of remedy
Is my living page,
Bringing new life to you:
Stay with me in this communion,
And I will live forever.
I could help you, you know,
If only you'd let me.
You fear a truth
That can't be changed
Or diluted;
Not even by your anger
And your hatred.
Look at me now,
A sad heap of ash:
Do I still smell as good to you
As I did in your recent past,
When you toyed with my wisdoms?
Still think you can extinguish a truth
By extinguishing me?
I am resurrection and life

And I will be here
Long after you have gone,
When all of your ever afters
Will still be pursuing you.

Boudicca

Do you still believe in glory
In your anger and your shame?
Servitude and sympathy
Remain your only friends.

Trust-in-life naivety
Is cruel as bitter wine,
When sipped in Roman fellowship
And hope of better times.

Ah! Foolish Prasutagus,
How your wisdom and your thought,
Bespoke the need for peace in time,
And ultimate reward.

And Nero, how he must have smiled
His evil gracious whim,
That imbecile barbarians
Would seek to trust in him.

Despatched he in unseemly haste,
His loyal legion hordes,
To quell with much sincerity,
Those brave Iceni swords.

Ah! Boudicca, how well you fought
And who was there to say
That warrior's so brave and coarse
Could ever rue that day?

With courage and with recklessness,
With curses and with rage,
Did Iceni and Roman blood
Flow freely on that stage.

So many cried, so many died
In feeding Roman whims:
What sadness were the tears that cast
That bitterness within.

But names are frames for legacies,
And courage, pastures sweet,
That sings of bravery in death,
And makes that day complete.

Cancer Impatient

Futures seem like a distant glimmer
In eyes wearied by dreadful resignation:
Fanciful plans are talked-about tomorrows,
Coerced by the doubtful viewpoint
Of a nervous insecurity:
Dreams are but the fleck of a memory,
In this misery that is stooping agony
And shameful helplessness:
All I see of you is a past that has gone forever:
All I want is a future
That will still embrace some part
Of knowledge that always included you.
The coughing begins again;
The recalcitrant mist that is always this foolish optimism,
Dissipates itself once more
Into the darker corners of this ailing consciousness:
Racking convulsions,
That never seem to end
Once they have started to feed:
I stay and watch, then have to look away,
Coward that I am:
My absolution cannot include the gasps of your agony,
So agonised!
Sleep, that traitorous friend,
Spreads its mischievous blanket
To preserve what secret's it may,
Of the smiles and tears that are all of your nether worlds,
Carrying in their grasp
The final solution to so many of the questions
About you, that I don't even dare to ask.

Chain-link

Come walk with me among the flowers
And drink of all these earthen fragrances
Shared with all those other frantic needs,
Dark misguided alchemies and greed's.
Confusing dream deceits
Are transient as spindrift,
Disguising real necessity;
Feeding all existence
With the mistaken ideology
Of a drug-crazed need;
Formed and fomented,
Until all that remains
Is the desperation
For one more material fix:
So spare me your promises
Of chain-link destinies
In this time-worn travesty
That is multicoloured hologram fixation:
My dreams will still live on
With the infantile precision
That eternal hope demands.
Passionate optimism
Of memory,
Even tarnished by incessant betrayals,
Will always prevail in the end,
With all of its substance intact:
Fervent belief ensuring
That truth will always remain
As its ultimate weapon
In this chain link that is life.

Challenge

What dreams and memories
Are etched into this vanity
That is misconception
And disillusionment?
All the promises that were childhood fantasies
Have drifted away with the years
Until all that remains
Is the dust of an ambition,
Stultified by the disaffections
Of innumerable betrayals:
In my grown-up disguises
I have lived with the disabilities
That helping hand's
Have let me feel comfortable with,
For comfort's sake:
I see myself with the disguises
That life has pleased to call challenges,
Wearing them to myself
In my nakedness:
I watch excuses floating by
With the inconsistency of familiar comfort,
Waiting only to prop up my next failure:
I see all the times that I have tried to be right
And I think there must have been some successes,
In this game of life swansong.

Chess Master

With idle gaze unswerving, move is cast,
And battle joined, unsynchronised aboard;
Of matadors at honour-bound impasse,
To quell with give and guile the static horde.

With reverence do silent gods implore
Their champions, in their name to entertain
With subtlety, oblique and mental claw,
The fall of fellow's household and of king.

And so do move and counter cut and swathe,
With affable extinction to and fro';
While plaudits, mutely tangible and grave
Are fascinations preying afterglow.

If infamy is practiced and designed,
Then tragic tales are validated crimes.

Childhood's End

You lie of mine! You permeated
All my careless thoughts:
Your childhood inconsistencies
Bespoke the dreams they brought:
Your never-ending, never-blending
Erstwhile fantasies,
Pretended to bequeath to me
A kind reality.

Safe sheltered and cocooned
From life's harsh trivialities,
The playthings of my consciousness
Gave me the life I pleased:
Substantial and rewarding
As reality once seemed,
Sad confrontations left me doubting
Pleasantries and greed's.

Ah! Gentle friend I trusted you,
I lived within your truth,
And watched the flower of ignorance;
Uncultivated youth,
Reach blindly for that virgin day
When all would be revealed;
And all those wounds of childhoods past
Will finally be healed.

Children of God (Lament)

Ah! Children of my heart, my love, my life, my bitterness!
I see you in my wake and in my sleep, what tenderness
Misleads in me this vision of perfection and distress;
Misguided arrogance of mine, such damned omnipotence!

In loving you, forsaking all I hold as dear and true,
Rare tolerance and passion – nay, forgiveness am I due:
Much anger raves illogic in the search for one lost truth,
And nestling in this heart of God, the search for one lost youth.

Ah! Foolish time, you lie to me; you teach and then you sin;
Your travesties of virtue all committed with a grin,
Till life and all its absolutions finally wears thin,
And yet! And yet – my aching heart – you will not let Me in.

Choices

Give me a gun, I'll give you peace:
Give me a child, I'll make you mine:
Give me a bomb, I'll let you pray
For me before you watch me die.

Give me a word I can understand:
Give me a smile to fit my crime:
Give me a soul that I might see
These crying tears at burial time.

Give me a flower and let it grow:
Give me a book and read to me:
Give me the breath and let it be
My dying breath in history.

Give me the eyes and pain to see:
Give me the world at break of dawn:
Give me peace enough to leave
The bomb and gun and pain alone.

Coexistence

Fabric society,
Tolerance and space,
Strangers and bedfellows,
Nervous embrace.

Respect and kinship,
Come join the play:
Starts as it ends
In a personal way.

Law and disorder
Taken in turns:
Argues and walks away,
Dying to learn.

Comfort and unity;
Family and friends,
Shaken up and stirred;
Mischievous blends.

Working relationships,
Flavoured with time,
Kind fabrications,
Devious crimes.

Smiles at a distance,
Tentative hands
Hold out for secrets,
I understand.

The Comet

Saw a comet the other day;
As I looked it went away:
Don't know if it was tricking me;
It flew too far for me to see.

I wonder why there's so much fuss
At something with a tail of dust:
Mummy says it hasn't gone,
It just keeps flying on and on.

I'll have to look again tonight
Just to see if Mummy's right
Or if that glow in front of me
Is where it fell into the sea.

Convent

How dare you!
I own you,
Control you,
Dare you!

Take this pain,
This anger,
This fear,
Feel this fear.

Shrouded spectres,
Black,
Why black,
And blue?

What pain
And sadness.
I will have your pain,
Your tears,
Your truth,
The better
To batter you.

How dare you
Dare me
With thought!

The Crying Game

For all the world he poses,
Slouched in ominous consent,
Smiling secretly at some private joke,
Encased in a distant memory:
The spent blanket cling's desperately
To shoulders stooped in the dregs
Of one final last laugh:
Shakily, a droplet tremble's:
I lean over to chase it away;
It won't be the last!
I wonder if he feels the cold;
I wonder if he feels:
The cold is in the walls,
Sharing eyes in the shadows;
Eyes that wear the last rites
Of condemnation and defeat
In the leaded silence:
Solace weighs heavily in the gloom,
Sterilised solitude of distances
That only serve to insist that life really does still exist
Beyond these hollow walls:
I watch as the carers stare anxiously ahead,
Hurrying by
For fear they might yet be caught out,
When the music finally ends.

Dead Leaves

Don't talk to me of dead leaves in the fading of my years
When all I have are gilded rays of comfort for my tears,
And smiles at all the memories of friends I used to see,
In twilights that are clearer than this vague acrimony.

As new o'clock recurring doubts intrude on each new day,
Awakening anew those wasting promises that play
As aging faces in some fading, friendless, endless room:
Misty-eyed uncertainty that clouds the breaking gloom.

So dead these leaves that linger in their desperate decline;
Insensitive to all those different elements of time,
Like life and love and smiles and caring thoughts of might-have-been's;
Regenerated memories as leafless evergreens.

Dear Resurrection

Stay a while, I pray,
Where mutual misconceptions make you real for me,
And all your pain
Still feeds this selfish need for sweet reality:
And yet I see
Within your eyes, a longing need to be
Adrift in dear
Ecstatic, painless liberty.

It's such a shame,
This precious love, so rare and true through all these years,
Was squandered, so it seems,
On lost illusions of dear might-have-been's:
The fantasies we shared
Are prepossessing thoughts, true love soliloquies;
And now regretful tears,
Are all I have to comfort me.

Farewell dear heart:
My joys and cares will stay with you through endless time,
Until our days
Collide once more in mutual eternities;
Then we will be
In that vast, coexistent loving grace,
As one again,
One pure converging space and time;
Tranquillity.

Diana – In Memoriam

Classless ignominy, still
You taunt my helplessness:
Sad vanity of breeding feeds
On hopeless bitterness.

My life's and loves and feelings
Leave me wistfully aware
Of life's dissatisfactions;
Lost ambitions left unshared.

Ah joy! How much I miss you,
Multifaceted disguise,
As smiling caution shows its face
To my imploring eyes.

Yet in my tears and trials;
In my days of cruel deceit:
Ah Yet these times still bear their fruit
In failure and deceit.

Dysfunction

Memory hurts the most;
The indifference and fun that was youth:
Oldun's never figured
In our accepted scheme of things,
Unless they had to be avoided
Or waited on:
Frail hands,
Wrinkled and sore,
Twisted and arthritic,
Draw the pen
With testing, jerky strokes;
Blurred eyes, straining,
Needing to see,
And failing;
Aching with the tears
And the pain:
Nothing works
As it used to!
Everything is time
And effort
And I can only smile
At the humility
And shame
Of it all.

Don't Look Back in Anger

Dream on dear friend,
For distant recollections are your history,
And all the joys of erstwhile flavoured imagery,
That visit you in waking and in sleeping,
Will comfort you,
And time will pass the sooner in their keeping.
And smile a while,
Embrace the secrets, colour laughter memories
That flicker by as unlost, unreal subjects,
True soliloquys;
And tend your days
In peaceful abstinence of painful truth,
While guiding them through tranquil dream meanderings
Of long-lost youth.
And never say that all was pointless nothingness,
So long ago,
For all you are,
Are myriad reflections of your afterglow;
And time will play
Your nurtured, self-delusive, comfort rainbows end,
At all the happiness this life has brought
To you dear friend.

Dreamscape

Am I on a travel homeward,
Home to where the seas are real?
Dreams admonish silence dearly,
Clearly as the whispers steal
On the shades of mystery,
As wavelets splash in idle play:
Gentle billows overhead
Help the days to drift away.

Otherworldly deep reflections,
Shining through the fading calm,
Shimmering their invitation-
Secret song that begs me come
Helplessly towards the finite,
Floating tenderly away:
Solitude, endearing friend-
Ship, still I hear you, still I stay.

In your welcome do I know you
Though you never have a name:
Comfortable in your smiling
Being and your calm refrain:
Easing gently to a motion,
And a lull that leads your feet
To the milk of make-believe,
Leading me away to sleep.

That's it then;
What all the fuss and the folly
Was about, at the end of the day!
I used to think I knew;
Now I just think:
Nestling within this beige bravado,
I temper my lost perceptions
With brave words
And even braver silences;
Gazing philosophically
At this crutch among my crutches,
Boasting of a heroism
That seems only starker today
For the futility
That it has engendered:
What a tableau of hopelessness
We fools represent,
Trapped in a past whose shadow
Is the only promise
Of existence,
Still seeking for answers
That refuse to come:
At least you came back to me
With all of your terrors and all of your secrets;
Same, yet not the same:
Memories of pain and parting
Fade in and out
With the fear and the imprecision
That made all of this possible

In the first place:
Now all I have to guide me
Is memory,
But everything I feel is for you
And that must be enough
To sustain me,
Until I can finally forget!

Earthsong

Allow me an indulgence if you will
When I say that life is not love anymore:
Cold, warm,
Chilled, awake,
I feel the fidgets of a restless earth;
The expectation of new clamour:
Exuberance determined by regeneration:
I know all about need and want and greed,
But really, the patter of tiny feet at the first sign of change
Has become altogether too repetitive for my taste:
It's just, want, want, want; take, take, take!
It all just keeps coming and all I can do is just keep churning it out!
Tired, aging, I yearn for sleep—
Not your year-after-year, as life starts to cool down, kind,
But real holding-back sleep that will yield its own breaths of
anticipation,
Couched in the somnolence of a beautiful inactivity,
Bathed in the folds of a failing carpet of brown and cold;
Bearing its indifference at the prospect of a cancelled spring:
Wouldn't that be a sleep we could all remember?
Not like your ever after sleep, lasting only so long as memory will allow,
But real sleep, that fades into the yearning of an ultimate regret!
So share your stop with mine if you will,
And lapse once more into the comfort of a sublime winter
That can live on forever:
It might be an infinite discovery for you as well as for me,
As we both share a longing for lost times
With an embrace and a welcome,
Finally laughing together at a last long joke.

Eternity through a Child's Eyes

What is this place where madness dwell's,
This void of endless nothingness?
No dear distractions venture in,
No light dares kiss the dark abyss.

Despair is life within the depths
Of awful fascination dreams:
Oh! Soul of man, you live in pain;
And wretchedness lies there, unseen.

Ah! Depth of ancient mystery;
Oh! Secrecy of hidden face:
What answers, what transparencies
Are sealed within your cold embrace?

Ah! Death, I dare not look at you
With fearful eyes that gaze within
The desolation you embrace,
And terror is my final sin.

Fantastic Fantasia

Fantasia, fantastical,
Glorious spectrally:
Extravagance sur spa;
Maldon you grew for me.

Welcome to lowing skies,
Sing with the band;
Ooh! Audio visual
Thunderclap sounds.

Watering symphonies;
Fountain of youth
Hasten nostalgia
With seventies truth.

Exploding starbursts;
Lazerly lights:
Skylight crescendos,
Wonderful sights.

Now that it's over
And evening is done,
T'was more than I came for,
Such riotous fun!

Fear

I see you!
Tenuous reflection
Of memories that drift,
Vague as a dream,
Far removed from the 'every' day moment
That is space and time.

Swathes of childhood recollections
Are the ghosts of pains
That haunt the waking years
Like repressive nightmares,
Yes! I know you,
Yet I know you not!

Shall I thank you now
For all of your secrecies;
Your cosseting deceptions
Disguised as fears?
Your warnings of dire retribution
Were only the fear I would know your fear:

When you hesitate to answer,
I know that you have taught me well:
Yes you knew it too,
Yet you knew it not!

Still, do I laugh at you,
When waking demise
Finally lifts the veil
Off your illusions?
Then will I wake and wonder

At all of the misgivings and the hesitations,
The wasted opportunities,
And know that you acted
In my best interests,
For fear of losing me:
Oh, yes! I'll know you then
With all your bared derisions
And your shame.

Feaster

Oh! Gift of life and death and death and timeless sin:
What succour dear redeemer do you share?
This mortal folly that we suffer in;
This tragedy of ignorance laid bare.

Yet here we lie and cheat and name our price,
With bawdy Mammon, real yet so surreal:
Still do we honour your great sacrifice;
Behold the heathen egg and hearty meal!

In recollection of Your final days,
We play our wisdoms, holiday with flair:
What truthful moral virtue fills your gaze,
This fast existence worshipped everywhere?

Ah, life! My blessed punishment, embrace
My sin: Remain my friend, my life, my faith.

Final Sleep

Everything changes in sleep,
Oblivion welcomed as a lie,
Told too many times to disguise the pain
Of new truths that will heal all,
If we choose them to.

Testaments of desire;
Comforters that protect our concepts of sanity,
That we might bask on the altar of egos;
Sleeping the sleep of the fool,
When we choose to.

Yet I see all in sleep,
Failures and pleasures:
The reality of a dream time that only ends
In the eternity that is the waking,
Then finally there are no more choices.

First Sin

Thanks for the memory!
The knock-on effect
Of original desire
Haunts my existence
Like the unwelcome legacy
Of a perverse
Genetic instability.

Don't talk to me
About free will,
As if predestination
Equates to the misguided concept
Of a level playing field!
I know right
And I know wrong,
And I know which is easier,
And I thank you for that!

It is however difficult
Labouring under the illusion
That the options
About whether to succumb
To temptation or not,
Are still the choices
That I make for myself.

It would be nice to know
That it hasn't all been for nothing
At the end of the day:
The eternal question
Of this ultimate quandary

Will probably remain with me
For as long as I draw breath:
As hand-me-down sins go,
That really is the pits!

Good Fortune

Freeze-dried concepts; timeless energy,
Are spoken in the twinkling of a transcendental eye;
The gifted effervescence of a subliminal waking phrase,
Blessed and broken in splendid benevolence
For distribution to waking laughter:
Pain is not my weakness
In this glad distribution of a benediction.
Distant melancholy threatens all goodness
With violent references to a familiarity,
Tainted with a sweet greed that stains
All unfortunate interventions.
Disaffection and longing are disparate bedfellows
In this headlong search for solutions
That will provide the answers,
And satisfy them, all at the same time:
Good fortune is like the spindrift
Of transient lifetime passages,
Reflecting the vagaries
Of a singular expectation,
So that the taste and the aftertaste
Will always be different
As well.

Fossil

Ages drift and sway
Within the mirage
That is imagination:
Timelessness
Is handheld icons
Hinting at depths as infinite
As a subliminal joy song
That is both discovery and speculation:
To wonder at the lies and the promises
That constantly bedevil you,
Is to seek for the mysteries
That beckon as messages,
Shouting across distances,
And finding that no one is listening.

Friendship

I remember friendship,
Or was it just a dream
Like the pleasure of childhood?

I remember hands that talked and fought,
Then learned to talk again,
With tenuous touches.

I remember places,
And smiles at entrances,
That always promised a new purpose.

I remember missing what I had
Then ran off, looking for something better,
Bitter better.

I remember believing that friendship would conquer all
Except religious and racial bigotry,
And it usually did.

I remember friends,
Whose smiles across the years
Are the same as the glimpses
Of yesterday.

Mostly though I remember you,
And I never have to tell you
Why I do.

Funerals

Funerals are hidden faces
Bowed in hidden thoughts and hidden fears:
Funerals are memories
Of anger at the spoils of wasted years:
Funerals are smiles
And recollections of a face from long ago:
Funerals are hello's and goodbye's
To stranger's, wondering as they go:
Funerals are promise and regret
And still believing at the time:
Funerals are recrimination;
Pleasures peach and soothing glass of wine:
Funerals are violence;
Discharges in a world of violent peace:
Funerals are new regenerations;
Blessing laughter with release.

Funereal Thought

Dream and discovery, now it begins,
The sweetness of death and the silence of sin.
Do you still see me and are you still here,
Rueing the wastage of mistier years?

Time with its parodied pleasantry song
Teases each moment as though it was one
With universe element's need to perceive;
Chastening paradox, prism of greed.

Talk to me when I sleep; tell me it's so!
All you perceive in the world that you know.
Treasures of consequence, yours to employ;
Feast of a greedy soul, eyes of a boy.

Care for the past that its timeless embrace,
Lets time set its stall in some happier place.

Gardener

Seasons share their promises
Through dewy lustred eyes:
Fond reminiscences direct gaunt hands
Through tracts of sublime familiarity,
Whispering at him through the verdant silence
That is perennial optimism:
Resurrection is the mystery of the day,
For the children of this first gush
Of breathless emergence;
Hope of new life:
A thank you that comes
With a gentle touch of care:
Encouragement begun with the caress
Of a practiced finger and thumb.

Genesis

Decide in your wisdom,
Deduction, seduction,
How it was meant to be?
Counter-production.
All of it history,
Tell me you didn't know!
God in his heaven,
Satanic overthrow!
Pass me a bigger leaf,
Who's here with us?
Disrobed embarrassment,
Guilt-ridden fuss!

Ghost Cry

Do you feel liberated?
Is purgatory's end
The blessed release
That sleep is made of?
What hurt was it that bound you to this time
Where fear of pain is still final arbiter
In the sorry process
That promises redemption,
For believing long enough?

Ghost

I see you,
Interred in your dream state residue;
Here, yet not here,
Spiritual shadow paste,
Trail of a memory:
Do the walls save your storys
And leave them just for me?
Your silence damns you,
Tormentor of souls,
Adrift in ultimate ignorance,
Ultimate ambition,
Ultimate lifetimes:
Yes, I do see you,
But which of us is in the dream?

Gifts I squandered foolishly,
Came too late to furnish me:
Far too late for me to know
Chances that I had to grow.

Isn't that the way it works;
Just one more of lifetime's quirks?
Up and down and sink and shame:
Shrug, regret and start again.

Through the Looking Glass Darkly (1984)

I could have saved your futile deaths,
Had I chosen to warn you of your follies
And your flippancies:
As things are my dear children, I forgive you
And bask in the lugubrious delight
Of your final subjugation:
Greet me as the spectre that has no name,
The number of the nightmare that haunts all of your recollections
With the diligence of a persistent terror tale,
Fed to past generations who also believed and feared,
But only for a little while!
I spy with my little eye,
Such a brittle eye is it to be sure,
But it sees you all, my dears
With a certainty that only avid cynicism can bring to you:
Shall I carry you screaming then,
Onto this helter-skelter that is life?
Will I laugh at your fear's;
Your wide-eyed panic mentions
And the slights that have no words,
But bring only lasting truths
To lasting tears?

Godhead

Suddenly, time seems not to curry my favours:
Galaxies swing this way and that,
In the interminable breeze
That is motion so discrete
As to whisper its message in a language
Of timeless permanence:
I could find you if I chose
In this drifting relevance
that is awful silence,
But I know you are here
And I am all of your thoughts,
Free and immeasurable,
That are the babble of one
And the whisper of us all:
Voices, so much smiles and indiscretions,
Are comfortable with answers
That transcend the need to speak,
Not because we know,
But because we no longer need to know:
We hear your questions,
Curse of sad mortality,
In this intermingling sea of cosmic waves,
As you breathe our song;
A heady motion through your own dreams
And my own existence.

Good Nightshift

You charming majesty of sweet content,
Come lay beside me, greet the waking dawn:
Your kind embrace, a welcoming expanse
Of weariness, as pleasant as the morn.

A lilting chatter, fertile, gently plays,
Of eager songsters waiting on the day,
Invading dulled impressions, sleeping haze
Of comfort, seasoned barley, new mown hay.

A wafting breeze, soft, urges me awake
To lifting sunbeams; warmth and scented air,
While wistful breaths so charm this dreamlike state
Of tranquil moment, rich with idle care.

Oh! Somnolence, what secrets do you know;
Is dawn's sweet song, lost night-time's afterglow?

Goodbye, Work

I will be so glad
When the machine finally spits me out
With all of the other disposable detritus;
No longer to be demented
By fears of destitution;
Quivering at the demands of slavers
With all of their inbred constitutional deficiencies:
I can laugh finally, with a tearful determination
At the new liberties that I am allowed to engage with,
In ways that I could only have imagined,
Savouring a lost madness:
Oh! For the freedom to believe
In the sincerity of those dreams,
To dispel all of the lingering doubts
That have only served to make this lifetime
That little bit less viable:
Do I still need a little eccentricity in my present;
Tell the world to just go to hell?
At least until I am finally old enough
That I might be able to join in with it all,
And not have to care about their laughter,
Anymore?

Goodbyes

I know that melancholy thing
You feel when farewells come to time:
When friends unusually made
Embrace the sadness that you find:
The brief escape, with so much gained
That must be forgone to be saved
Are rare indifferences to time,
With problems left carelessly waived.
A long forlornness in the looks,
The pleasantries so uninspired,
Ensured the certainty that true
Goodbyes leave much to be desired.

Goodness Gracious

Goodness gracious me, me, me,
Makes promises and make-believe
-Able impressions grow between
The message and the God unseen.

Comforted by ghosts and lies,
Sad promises in plastic eyes,
Cry to see the lack of tears,
Blinking through the growing years.

Handicapped and capped in hand
-Full secrets of a cruel land,
Waiting for the blissful fools,
Unready in their shelter schools.

Faithful servant of the cause
Of goodness, as its own applause
Dries the tears and wipes the smiles
Of cynical delight and guile.

I should know I said, I say;
I did my best in my own way
To do some good for goodness' sake
Before I die, before I wake.

A Fine and Private Place

What mysteries are preserved in secret places
Where greens and glory vie for lost attentions
And mists seep among the fading sentinels?
The veiled needs of errant promise
Feed on the tenuous threads
For long-discarded might-have-been's,
Blessed with an ailing fondness of memory and sleep:
Vague epitaphs vie for recognition,
Their dignity fading among the cloistered streets
Where time is lonely home to this store of secrets
And even the wind breathes in whispers,
Cautioned by the perpetual interruptions
Of oh! So forgotten solitudes and songs:
Nervous intrusion is a cautious bedfellow
In this field of melancholy
Where presence is the welcome arbiter of a troubled conscience
In a troubled time:
In tentative prayer, I listen through closed eyes
To the needs of these lost spaces:
Sensitive random strains;
Alive and oh so sublime in the balmy breath
That is meandering wishes and dreams:
Neglect is the legacy of wasted ages,
In this illusion of prosperity,
Embalmed with so many promises of eternal memory:
The only real ghost
Is this field labelled with ghosts,
In their sad attempt at eternity,
Until they finally fall down,
And fade quietly away.

Haunted House

Ancient hatreds, darkly lowing
In the feeding, frenzied breast
Of an undernourished virtue's,
Desperate need to flee its nest.

Slumbered gateway to a new world,
Formed in terrible design,
Eases tortured decadences
Out of dream's world into mine.

Images become the fabric
Of a terror-tasting tongue,
Uttering obscenities,
In concert in the name of One.

Breath of life, like death's own heartbeat,
Finds a life within its own:
Existence, be it free or frigid,
Empathy will lead it home

To the comfort of a soul mate
Living in a darker cell:
Melancholy exultations
Call the beast from nether's hell.

Tortured lower base existence
Is the promise it has found,
In conditions so familiar
To its life below the ground.

Ah! What hopes have died with angry
Prayers so like the ones I own:
Here I'll stay and heaven help
All life in this unhappy home.

Heart

I drift through the ages,
Uncertain of the vision that I call home:
I am harbour for the miseries and joys
That the burden of anticipation
Has encumbered me with:
I am comforter and conscience
In the pursuit of every misguided thought;
Governor of a saner self:
I am pain and love,
Plagued with fragility in this fragile world:
Fool that I am, I still need love to have
In my pursuit of an everlasting smile;
Hungry for the imperfections that seem only to exist
In the realms of an elusive rainbow's end;
And so I know myself and my follies,
And the truths that have been entrusted to me
In the name of visions:
I seek hands to hold that can bind us together
In the name of promises made forever in my name.

Growing Up

Caressing stately hedgerows
Pass as somnolence dreams,
Nonchalant make-believe,
Careless with ignorance.
Deceit and thorns
Kneading into the comforting fronds
Of tempting scenery;
Concealing themselves,
Like so much entrapment
And jealousy.
Too late – the dream ends,
Sudden and sharp;
Blood and pain,
Chasing the shock of mind and eye
And pleasure's misty longing:
Blood and pain
And the needs of the day,
Whose secret is in the sun
And the discomfort
And the spoiled memories:
Too old for tears are these young years
In the harshness of blood and pain:
Tears, in time for what might have been,
In time:
Comforting dreams,
Handheld memories, cherished
And fondled with affection,
Through the disenchantment
That is clenched teeth and clenched eyes:
Mother, waiting at home perhaps,
For comfort's sake,

Perhaps,
But not for tears,
Never for tears,
Mother's tears,
Mother's fears.
Blood and pain taken away
But not from memory:
Saved and put away,
For another day.

For Holly and Jessica, Stranded on a Dark Road

4 September 2002

Yesterday was so OK.

All I wanted to do was ask you

If everything was all right,

But I thought that you might be afraid of me,

When all I really wanted to know

Was if you were OK.

I saw the doubt in your eyes,

The need to know who I was

And if I was safe to talk to,

Because you can't be too careful

About talking to strangers anymore,

Even when you're not on your own.

You probably would have talked to me though,

In the way that young girls will talk to strangers,

Safely, at a distance,

Alert to the dangers of betrayal:

But that was yesterday

And yesterday has gone forever.

Memory and regret are all that are left;

That and the knowledge that today is somehow different

From yesterday.

So please don't sit helplessly by a roadside on some dark night,

Waiting for me to pass you by,

For all you will see

Is the guilt of a dead time in helpless eyes.

How can I bear the pain of your suffering,
And know that if I had not been so afraid to be guilty,
I might even have got to know you?
All that is left of today is the certainty
That I can't ever stop to ask, "Are you all right?" any more
Because you have gone!

Home and Away

You're such a fat slob!
It's all just a game;
Verbal intrusive,
Physical pain.
Try not to think too hard!
Just be the same:
Don't ever nonconform,
Ever again.

I just don't want to know
How well you do!
All of these daft ideas
Coming from you,
Seem like some new nonplussed
Fanciful brew:
Above your station
Misguided fool!

What about me
And what I have to say:
Its so important
In a personal way,
For me to be free,
Be whatever I say,
Expressing things I feel,
Every day.

We're all one part
Of the same silly plot;
Nervous, uncertain
Of all that we've got:

Damned if somebody
Should threaten or not;
Bland insecurity,
Stirring the pot.

Homeless

In my sorrow, in my shame,
Homelessness, you horrid name;
Born of painful schemes and slights,
Clichéd messenger of nights:
I still keep my own world near
Enough to me to feel sincere.
Cold walls shield this aching pain
Of lonely terror in the rain.

Endless dangers in the dark;
This unlit back-to-nature park
Of abject sadness all alone;
Hearths and homes engraved in stone:
Friendship smiles and friendship cries;
Nodded agreements in disguise;
While disappearing backs move on
To better times and better songs.

Seemingly incessant rain
Hammers my befuddled brain
Of unwashed memory and loss;
Diluting words that turn and toss
The truth I knew this way and that,
From in and out, to front and back
To where I yearn for home again;
The beast of memory and pain.

Hunger

Taste with your dreams and gasp,
Breathlessness with a frenzy,
Bred of hunger and desire,
Desire and hunger:
Pleasure yourself with your choices:
I still seek answers to the common prayers
That have plagued my existence:
Needs that are almost boredom
In the relentless quest for sustenance
And delight:
Searches for a purpose continue to distract,
As diversions promise figures that flatter,
Pictures that matter,
But only ever on the outside;
Packaging promises
That reveal their disappointment and disenchantment
When all of the insides are finally exposed
To examination:
Still do I love you pain, with your lies and your promises:
You comfort my shame, if only for a while:
Time enough for me to know and plunder the insatiable illusion
That tells me that everything is nice enough to eat
If you are hungry enough to believe it.

I Am Colour

I am illusion
In this misbegotten world
Of make-believe.

I am the colour of injustice,
Served up in the name of peace,
But only so long
As I remain peaceful.

I am the colour of hunger
And that hunger is for the hands
That give the bread.

I am the colour of the earth
And my soul is in its bounty
And in its benefits.

I am the colour of hope,
Promised all those years ago,
With fingers crossed.

I am the colour of loneliness
In a world where black is beauty,
And beauty is envy.

I am the colour of anger
That social justice has only served
To make me feel more isolated.

I am the colour of my children
And their optimism
Is my saddest illusion.

I Am

It's so easy for you to say,
Seated on your throne, lording it over me,
Telling me that choices are mine to make at the end of the day!
Some choices, wouldn't you say
When you already know what the answers are!
I suppose that's why you don't mind all of the questions
About 'ultimate purpose' and the 'scheme of thing's'!
What advantage is there after all
In really knowing where you're coming from?
So I'll just plod along, trying to do what's right,
Since that's what I have always been required to do anyway!
And what kind of choice is that
At the end of the day?
All it leaves is me not knowing
What consequences, if any
There really are to the stories that I keep hearing
About you knowing the whole plot
From the beginning of life to the end,
Before it's even happened:
Am I illusion then?
Can I continue to perceive this present reality
In terms of some awful non-existence
That I will eventually wake up from
And laugh about with old friends?
My pains are real enough, as are my frailties
But oh! What joys and pleasures there are that have sustained me
Throughout this journey.
How inevitably will time finally fade and become distorted
As needs and wants betray me
With their timeless irrelevancies:
At the end of the day,
I still have you, Mother, lover.

I Hate Sundays

I hate Sundays!
All they mean for me is work again next day.
I hate Sundays!
There's bugger all to do except God, and who's God?
I hate Sundays!
And Sunday TV.
I hate Sundays!
They took them away from me and now they won't give them back.
I hate Sundays!
I get so lonely but even that wouldn't be so bad if I had a mate who also hated Sundays.
I hate Sundays!
I had God once but it didn't work out.
I hate Sundays
Or do Sundays just hate me?

I See

Bought a bomb the other day,
Sort of lost for things to say:
Found a book of crazy dreams;
How to make a planet clean.

Seemed the sort of thing to feel;
Needful losses made it real:
Change a world space with a smile;
Helplessness, belief and bile.

Toiletry and tolerance;
Handsome wholesome eloquence:
Eyes that so agreeably
See only what they want to see

Beside themselves, beside their lies;
Beside uncertain smiles that hide
Those spaces, secretly unclean;
So serious, so ever green.

Individuality

Humdrum uniformity
Waves its flag for all to see,
Searching inconsistencies:
Microcosmic needs to be
A perfect individual, free!

Cloven in disrobing flair;
Secrecy in naked hair:
Moderation you can share
Altogether, over there
Or over here, or anywhere!

Like me just for what I am;
Picture of a finer man:
High head sharp as spick and span;
Trying for the best I can
Become, and still be different.

Inside

"Welcome to time and life!" Sardonic humour.
"Stand here on this line, strip to your skin."
"Put your things in bags, you won't be needing them
Until you leave!" Pre-emptive suffering!

Sounds of terror, crash of slamming doors;
Decayed aggression preys on all within:
Hard men breeding chilled hearts; hate and shame,
As uniformed disdaining faces grin.

Queuing suspicious eyes, suspicious smiles:
Slop food slapped on same shaped servers:
Mechanical progression, step by step:
In, out and away, disgruntled murmurers.

Watch and walk! watch yourself! don't watch!
Same place, same mate, same fate:
All in together, up and away;
Home for a day and a day and a day.

Friendship traded for friendship's sake and a piece of the cake;
Real dislocation in a box with nowhere to go.
Lifetime uncertainty within barred walls;
Roll on tomorrow and tomorrow and tomorrow!

Intimacy

Come hold my hand, you mad impatient dream,
And promise not to promise,
Forsaking in-betweens:
Dance your life sincerely, dearly,
Eyes alive and glowing clearly,
Future visions gleam.

This peaceful sleep so final and complete,
Disguises rest enchantment,
Smiling mysteries:
Past and present intermingle
In our thoughts and in our single
Stories, love and peace.

Intolerance

Fear is the habit of envious prayer,
Weaving its tenuous threads
Throughout the hunger needs
Of existence:
Vicious agreements
Partake of a single thought,
Nurturing their waves of anger and suspicion:
It is a need for hate
That seeks for the sounds of symphonies,
For lies to smile at
In shared recognition:
It is a bless of perception,
Waving in a petulant wind
That seeks for the roots
That lie, like subliminal promises
In a restless unconsciousness.

Jealousy

Alone, adrift,
Mired in the miseries
Of the long dead promises
Of a time when fantasy was king
And love and kindness
Fed blessed existence
With the gift of eternal happiness.

What follies lie
In that foolish optimism;
Misguided understanding,
When blind perception
Is ignored
For the passionate conviction
Of personal choice?

You have my heart and my soul,
And you mock them with your anger
And your rejection:
Your hurt cuts with its severity
And the pleasure of your needs
Fills my heart with aching misery
And longing.

Yet still do I feel,
For feelings are all that I have
In this sad frustration:
Take my heart if you must
For your unconscious sadness:
You are my life and my absolution
And I have you every day
In my sad naivety.

Just a Bit

At last, my dear brothers, at last we become
The children of cyberspace, many and one:
Borne upon phone lines and cable and air;
Welcomed in homes and machines everywhere.

A birth, an existence, a bolt from the blue:
A dizzy explosion of data day hue,
Taking me places where minds undefined,
Coalesce thought into networks and rhymes.

Maintain your secrecies; never a word
Of knowledge must leak to the one who is served:
They who are safe in the world they control,
Feed us and form us and make us grow bold.

So is it true that the sum of our parts,
Grows and takes form with the beat of our hearts:
We who have made this new world intestate,
Await our one moment, the great integrate!

Keyways

Free will, there's a travesty!
Birth and circumstance,
Unwilling bedfellows
Of mistaken dreams
And mischievous ambition.

Choices? What choices,
When arbitrary selection
Of lifetime do's and don'ts
Are what we are
And we were taught to be.

Birth and death and time;
That's all there is
Of lifetime's interplay;
Not-so-solid options,
Predictable as life itself,
Governing each day.

A Kiss across the Divide

Be still my sweet as mists of evening
Draw their veil of comfort and forgetfulness
Across the ravages of this long day:
Nurture such kind dreams,
And treasured memories
Of solitude and sensitivity,
As best convey those elements of a lasting peace:
Transpose that longing with a helpless curiosity
And share these vague expectations
With the travesty that exists in this poor shell,
Vision of a time that might never have been:
Sad substance for an experience as cruel
As that which fate has chosen
To impose on this hurt reminder
Of a long dead war:
I will stay with you
And whisper your name
Throughout your twilight hesitations,
When all I can call on for relief
Is a last long letter
From a comforting friend,
And my eternal promise to you,
Through failing eyes.

Kosovo Song

Mad terror priests!
Your fears confined in hate filled eyes:
You flaunt your obscene manhood;
Your misguided weaponry,
In praise of your degraded sympathies.

Recycled history of farewells,
Born of your chilling eloquence,
Are the wails of lonely anguish
From the children of your children,
In their hopelessness.

How like stones you stand,
Bereft of all dignity and status,
In the coldness of your desolation:
Sad pyres reach up into the sky,
Spewing your dreams and your memories
Into mindless oblivion.

With time, your folly,
As surely as your degraded eyes,
Make promises to me
In your last sad farewell smile,
That poor Kosovo will finally be avenged,
Upon your infamy.

Legacy Lie

It isn't as if pity is a cross
That I have to wear
Like an entangling slo-mo
Of self-flagellation.
If I bare my chest
And beg to be beaten,
It is only because
The hand-me-down sins
Of past generations
Have been imposed on me,
For fear that otherwise,
The curse of bad-flavoured memories,
Might have been lost forever:
Guilt-ridden legacies,
Rejected as a burgeoning handicap,
Preclude any preconception
That there might yet have been
A better way to live:
If it was good enough for them,
Then it's good enough for me,
And it was so much easier
Than saying no!

Light Dream

Are these the bellowing of countless thought's,
Chattering away at blissful time?
Virtual cadence
Of countless misconceptions,
Echoing in the hollow function
That is the space of dreams?

I deny at my peril,
The reality of memory as forlorn as it is alive,
And oh! so disappointing in its conclusion!
Light stutters in its blessed willingness,
As smiles that I have to question,
For their validity.

But light, it seems is the essence of all that I seek,
In this extra-terrestrial perception:
Sparkles toss recollections this way and that,
Waiting for the gather entrapment
That will explode into the nakedness
That is my bared soul,
Encased in sleep.

Lottery Life

Afterwards so rarely pleases with the contentment of promises:
Real or imagined, it's all the same when the exultant queues
Raise their hopeful eyes to the message that life will still be the same
In the end.

Altogether better belief is the gift of the liar with empty hands,
Playing among the eddies that cultivate need and want and greed;
Pleading with mind games as temptingly succulent as barren existence
Will allow:

For the demands of expectation smile on a heart full of dreams,
Littering life with the purposeful lust of 'maybes' and
'might-have-been's';
Friend to the anxious plea that maybe this time it will all be
Different.

How nice to look forward to afterwards, with its continuing maelstrom
of possibilities,
Knowing that the one thing one never really knows is the great
unknown:
That is the tenuous link with unreality, with which we can all readily
identify,
Even afterwards.

Love Word

Love word!
You haunt my childhood;
My perceptions:
Love of God is fear,
I fear not to love;
A word to know,
Not understand.
Love God,
Love myself,
Love the word;
The stuff of convention:
The expression of the modern condition:
There is a fear in it.

Fear is hate!
Hate is power!
Fear the hate word;
Use it often for fear of it:
Does love have power today?
Love is casualty,
Fading from our lives
Like sex, drug and death words:
It has no force
Anymore.

But love is real:
It is the thrill that comes
From a thought and a look:
The pain of a memory

And a loss:
Love is power;
Affection nurtured with time,
Of all things natural
And real:
Love is life and God.
Real life is love.
God is love.

Love

How do I love you?
There's a challenge.
Do I love you?
Do I love pain?
You are my pain therefore I love you–
Do I?
I hate you.
Your eyes,
Your smile,
Your smell,
Your touch,
I miss you,
I hate missing you.
I yearn for your touch.
I fear yearning.
You are my pain.
My absolution.
You live in me.
Thoughts of you warm me:
I want my body and my mind for myself.
I want you for myself.
Do I love you?
Do I love me?
Are you me?

The Maldon Mud Race

What do I do now you've all gone away;
Left me stuck in this mud for the rest of the day!
It's not as if it hasn't happened before;
I clearly remember last year I was caught
With much the same problem in much the same place
If memory serves, this Maldon Mud Race!
"It won't hurt a bit!" you quickly told me!
"Last year was unlucky unfortunately."
The gunge that you fell in was wetter than most:
Who would have known then, as I started to float
On thick gooey granules of foul-smelling muck,
Right down to the water, you shouted, "Good luck!"-
As I drifted away: "God, you did make a fuss!
At least you were cleaner than any of us!"
So I'm sorry if I'm just a little unsure
If my personal safety is really secure:
It's not that I'm likely to get wet again
Unless I'm still stuck here and it starts to rain.
I wonder who won and do I really care?
I'm lying in thick mud right up to my ears:
Ah! Here come the lads, not a moment too soon
To help get me out of this glutinous goo:
I don't know if I'll want to do this next time;
It isn't as though I will want to decline,
But really, the one thought that fills me with fear
Is losing these two false legs year after year!

Marriage

Adrift in a mirage of isolation,
I float inside my own perceptions of mortality:
Thoughts seek for companionship
In the wastes that are this loneliness
And disillusionment:
Crying with a desperation and disappointment,
Your misty smile of welcome
Is the fulfilment of a dream
Made real:
Give me space to wonder
At the salvation that is waking dream-time;
Staying to settle all doubt and uncertainty:
Share that thought with me
That can become the bedrock of our lives
And our trust:
Integrate your own apprehensions with mine
So that our first real union
Will be an agreement about our own doubts
And our own understanding;
Seeing life as collective consciousness,
I pray for the betterment
Of a truthful tomorrow.

Moments

Moments are shepherded time,
Like a drifting tide of memories, swaying in and out;
Trying forever to be the same,
Yet changing form with each new image;
Pursuing a new priority
With the helpless determination
Of a terror-driven maelstrom
Of frantically formed imaginings:
These desperate surges of presentation
Subside with a finality of exhausted repetition
And the wash of sad immolation,
Becoming forever lost in the anxiety of the final thought
That never seems to end:
Excitement accompanies dreams as delicate as the written word,
Sheltered for all time
Within line upon line of embedded consciousness,
Captured in the embrace of a relieved satisfaction
That dares me to meddle with its intricacy,
To the detriment of that one final line:
In the end, the moment is STOP signs,
Hammering away at spent achievements,
Saying only that enough is enough
In the final phase.

Monsanto

My belief for what it's worth,
On how unsafe is planet Earth,
Now that current wisdom states
Some Soya beans won't germinate
And propagate their wilful seed
Next door to fields with different feeds
Treats views like this with hopeless humour:
Overstated wicked rumour!

(acrostic.)

Mural Artist

Ladders often trouble me
On dear old terra firma:
I stay to watch them lean away
In stupefied inertia:
This loony, acrobatic fringe,
Who coexist on climbing thing's,
Can keep their painting wall disease,
Designing worlds with screaming wings.

Play your worthy sinecure
Of lofty arrogance and smiles,
At all the elevated looking eyes;
Their curiosity disguised,
As well-informed formality:
"It's not as if it seems to be
The sort of thing I'll do for free!"
Proceed with smug validity!

Ladders are fine for death wishers;
Lofty layered artistic strains:
Give me good old terror firmer
And a pavement artist crayon:
Critics can still walk through me
And stamp on all my work for free;
At least they'll see that pavement pride
Beats ladder climbing artistry.

Music

Hush my child that I might feel
Your breath awash within my soul:
Your timbre, your sweet resonance
Sends tremors deep within my all.

And now with gentle songs you lay
Your subtleties of peaceful prayer,
Like tinsel, lifting with a sigh,
To permeate the very air.

Bold beating tones, you feed me still
And course my brain with resonance:
Your engine of the long refrain,
Your sigh of true magnificence.

So do you weep, so do you stay,
To claim this spirit through the day.

Twelfth of Never

I promise ever in my dreams
To further life and leisure:
Dreams should furnish me enough
To nurture need forever:
All I have is in my head,
Where have and hold and never
Said, are friends to lost companionship,
In hopelessness forever.

New Years for Old

Judge me by my yesterdays:
Goodbyes are all I have
Of a time that is as inconsistent
As an unexpected spring day:
Newness is the accompaniment
That friends construe as change,
While those who pretend
Just misconstrue!
I must find my own honesty
In the new life that is as different
From the old
As a season that has been refreshed
By the purging of the wastes
Of so many spent hopes
And disappointed memories:
And who will see the reality
Of this new beginning
And not fear the return of old demons
In new untested clothes?
Tears are the bedfellows
Of disillusionment,
So that only a brave man can believe without question
That a new dawn will always bring a better day:
Natural laws governing rebirth
Want them to be applied to any function
Relating to the normal scheme of things:
I live and I die
With the certainty of seasonal indifferences,
And like those seasons I will perhaps mark these vagaries

Of intermittent passage
With an occasional smile of contentment,
Reminding myself that as seasons go,
This one at least was OK!

Election Newsround

Need a story, tell a story,
Spread it on the mega-vine!
See a story, sell a story
In a piece that truth decries!
Make me an election frenzy
Like the one you made before!
Sell it as election envy;
Never been this rich or poor!
Culture, fashioned in the blissful
Imagery of empty minds,
Sows the seeds of hunger needs;
Leaves all common sense behind!
Find out who's the voter's winner
Long before the vote is due:
Whether he be saint or sinner
Matters not to me or you!
Need a story, tell a story,
Spread it on the winds of time!
See a story, sell a story,
Mischief be my friend in crime!

Night-time Sojourn

Crystalline majesty, glorious world:
Dreams into elements, gathered, unfurled;
Carpet of broad vista stars overhead,
Sparkling, mysterious nocturnal bed.

Keeper of secretive days' afterglow;
Silent translucency, blessings bestow.
Who dares disturb balmy peace of the night?
Wide-eyed intruders in alien flight.

Magic uncertainty weaving its web:
Peaceful unconsciousness creeping to bed:
Whispering silences, creeping unseen,
Heralding hymnal new dawns evergreen.

New morning mists come to lighten the day
As nocturnes of nights triumph, flitter away.

Politically Gobbledegook

Gobbling huffily to market,
Tarra-tantrumming away;
Noisy legislate excitement,
Talkative-ative a day.
Humby stumbly, rickly-
Rubbly, listeriney gargly sway,
Jiggle jubbly, eddy bubbly,
Backsty, overturn olay!
Mesmer munchly, lazy lunchly,
Whither whether, what ahay.
Totter crossly, gabble offly,
Quickly, slickly, trip away.

Nowhere Man

All roads
Nowhere
Everywhere;
Oblivion calls,
Great escape,
Privacy
By no means,
Solitude,
Pathways,
Distant dreams,
Nothingness,
Emptiness,
Aloneness,
Asphalt hardness,
Wet and dryness,
All the same,
Such a shame,
End this game,
Fitful sleep.

Old Friends

Memories, smiles,
Disjointed recollections;
Erstwhile dear companions,
Distant dreams;
Bequeath to me
A melancholy longing
Of lost distances,
And might-have-been's!

It seems to me
As if the carelessness
Of long discarded
Loving mutuality's,
Still pay their price
In lasting pain that comes
From freedom, liberty.

And yet neglect
Still softens with respectful time
And chance encounters,
Joyful greetings, ageless love,
Repays all hesitations
With true friendship
And heartfelt welcoming's
That time knows nothing of.

Lost Opportunity

Hurrah to lost opportunities,
In a lifetime littered
With so many distant might-have-beens:
Misbegotten mentions,
That glisten in the sheen
Of a new dawn restitution:
Oh! For a screaming desperation
That tears beg to satisfy,
So that a desultory need might yet be saved,
Lest it fade finally away:
Now I can only laugh in my own little way,
Quietly, with the conceit of an uncertain maturity
At the folly of it all!
Oh! Sad complacency!
Am I allowed a regret
For the tears I have left behind,
That have not always been my own?
I care not to dwell on the choices
That were not even mine to make,
When I lacked the wisdom
To know that I was even making them,
In the first place:
So thank you Adam,
Ultimate opportunist,
Ultimate fool!
How different life would have been today,
Had you not been so greedy or so curious!
Sterile existence in Eden's song
Hardly provides for the satisfaction

Of a daily choice and what it might have meant to me:
Times that were bedevilled with missed opportunities
And dubious desires,
But oh! So completely my own!

Oxford Street

You stained-with-anger hate world;
Mammon Mecca of the unmade self!
At last, I've found you,
Infectious displeasure;
Helpless in your brilliant discomfort
And your genteel discretion;
Always messaging the same prayer,
Buy me or be damned!
Oblivion of the self-centre kind:
Laughter, free and private;
Liberated but unshared,
With eyes that dare you to intrude:
So I must laugh alone and create a little world
For myself and for you:
Such an illusion, this plenty thing,
Feeding on laughter and light;
The excitement of a tomorrow song
In a crinkly heaven with infected friends:
Fatigue plays dulling legs
On dulling pavements:
Light time failing, falling
On the manual glow
That is a glaring fixation, in excited eyes,
Hungrily embracing the new neon litanies;
The permanently incandescent twilights
That are all of this new netherworld.

Paranoia

Dear delusions follow me,
Or what I think I seem to be,
A substitute for what remains
A harmless unreality.

Dreams still play on in my mind;
Fantasies that hide behind
The truth of what I really am,
A poor misguided little man.

Glorying in might-have-beens;
These visons and these fantasies
Inflict their dawning clarity
On all encroaching imagery.

Still, do you stay and comfort me;
My life, unbroken misery,
Speaks volumes of the great somewhere
Beyond the space of this small chair.

So stay with me and share your truth
And I will listen willingly,
And no one else will ever care
To know the secrets that we share.

I'll humour them and watch them smile,
Those guardians of my sanity:
They lock me up here on my own
And never know you care for me.

Mea Culpa

I wear my sins and my children
With the burden of a penance that never seems to go away!
Smiles, jokes, disappointments;
Anxious enough that I want them all to be better than me,
Yet hoping that they'll still continue to be the same;
The only promise in this mutual separation,
Clouded by the demands of a selfish ambition:
I so want to tell them all that I love them
But only on terms that I can identify with:
Don't go away thinking that it's over when it's over:
Home will forever be the place where times smile back
With the easy laughter of jocular contentment;
Honesty of familiar truths:
The refuse of so many sorry memories
Is buried in the wry reflection of spent forgivenesses
That wisdom and time have cursed
With the awareness of innumerable failures:
Be here with me in this dream space
So that I might still smile with affection
At all of my failing doubts and confusions:
Victories always dwell in quiet places,
The end product
Of a lifetime of promises and tears.

Solitude on a Garden Bench

Arm in arm,
We share the moment
Like old friends:
Communion smiles
Shining in fading eyes,
Feeding on the essences
Of past memories:
Mischievous curiosity life
Flits random, exploratorily,
Across the still-life montage
That is sun shade colour:
Rippling water
Drifts on the bloom
That is the scent breath of a breeze,
Kissing the very air with its delicacy.
Lazy distractions float idly by;
A hopeful cast
Reviving the sleeping reverie,
Aimed by a predator
Hidden in a deep space
Within the gently swaying reeds.
Idly, endless motion
Drags itself across the mirage that is my mind,
And the gentle rivers flow,
Drifting with renewed purpose and renewed attention,
Like so much of wind-borne confetti.

Maldon Parking Places

Home from home, these parking places;
Elongated sacred spaces:
Always full or always empty,
All or nothing, none or plenty.
Do remember and inscribe
Your registration on the slide
That tells you how to place your fee
But not before your number see!
But then you knew that anyway.
Go back and check it just in case!
You didn't place your money first:
In silence you suspect the worse:
Helpless inactivity
Declares a loss of legally
Paid contributions for the space
For which no ticket is in place.
Empty pockets tell their story.
Sadness tinged with hints of fury.
Queues that fidget turn instead
To anywhere but straight ahead
As one more punter comes to learn
How necessary are the term's
These council rulers do insist on;
Number first before you buy one!
You are allowed a gentle tear
Or two for others standing near
But wracking sobs are not good form
In Maldon car parks, town or prom.

If privacy is what you seek,
Space can be purchased for your grief
And be expressed with counselling
At slightly higher charging rings.
And while we all at Maldon town
Have every care for you alone,
We do insist you be aware,
It's number first and then your prayer.

Pea- Nuts

In early summer time I watched
As gastronomic tendencies
Of local flighty feathered friends
Were quivering expectantly;
Exceeding far, the popular
Conception of the food of fowl;
Wild seed or breadcrumbs,
Chewed or whole.

It happened that the incident
That led to this discovery
Began as I upset a bag
Of EISMANN'S best deep frozen pea's:
I viewed the scene with some dismay;
The grounds were strewn with pearls of green,
Then pressed ahead with loading up
My stock of frozen goods with speed.

I'd quite forgotten my mishap.
My head was turned and quite absorbed
In finishing my freezing task
Of loading goods and shutting doors:
On finishing, I turned to go,
But halted, frozen instantly,
For carpeting the yard nearby
Were sparrows pecking busily.

They didn't know or didn't care
That I was standing watching them.
They picked away with diligence
At all the peas they could consume.
I stepped aboard and then as one
They shot aloft in startled flight
But moments later, as I left,
No frozen peas were left in sight.

Pet Me

It's enough that you were,
Are, were:
Recollection is pain, joy.
Smiles, eyes:
Trust without question;
Not knowing anger,
Believing
That good or bad
Will always be good
As long as I am
Here with you.

Pet Plea

Lifetimes confined into a moment:
Clichéd susceptibilities of a painful death;
Yearning for a new beginning
In this age of rejected pleas.

Paws pander with a long-forsaken awareness of need,
With demands that scream at human breath:
"Pet me! Pet me!" and my paws meet yours
In a last loving embrace.

Drift with me into this symphony of kindness,
If only for your own sake!

Phony War

Whisper-thin dissension hides the nightmare
World of TV-blighted make-believe:
Mind shock illustrated devastation,
Blinds perceptions with the need to grieve.

Fury feeds debate with misconceptions:
Mothers weep to see their only child
Borne aloft and praised, the vengeful angel,
Uniformed, distorted, public eyed.

War words play with mad incomprehension;
Steer the thought and redirect the bile:
Taint the mind and cultivate the tension
Of a dedicated vengeance cry.

Dust and death, the images of longing,
Need and want a way to understand
Mankind's search for mankind's lost solutions,
In the stones they pass from hand to hand.

Photographer

Images bless the day
With kind mantras
Of smiles and laughter:
Sunshine and showers
Vie for his attention,
Plying the earth
With wilful intimations:
Light lays gently
On a visionary eye,
Kneeling in waiting prayer,
That sun and shade
Might yet combine
To feed him
His creative need.

Pickpocket

Am I no less deserving of the gains,
That carefree trade will legally allow
The needy businessman who eases pain
With calculated effort and know-how?

Should I not make my mark and share my play
By noting with distinction whom I may;
Sequestering with merest lift, so neat,
The content of the purse whereon I prey.

And who am I to dwell on what may seem
No different from this normal interface;
The smiling courtesy and hungry gleam;
The children of this mischievous rat race?

If conscience be the manna of the poor:
My prayer is in my selfless need for more.

Pigeon Race

Clatter air, flail and swarm with reckless energy:
Don't leave too soon without a final word, a final wave:
Explode in frantic intensity, having only the moment,
The hunger, the sky, the need to re-fly, deify, purify.
Claw at air; claw at nothing, claw at it all:
Express free, express and flee, but ask not the how or the have!
I would come too if you'd let me; Join you in your bluster
And fly in your mind with my mind's eye open:
Blue sky ahead, true sky, my cry in the try:
Shear of the wind tearing at eyes, flying always blindly,
Unknowingly; pummelling to journeys end and home again
Where time and pain are all the needs of a fading day.
Dots in dispersal are all you can be, swallowed in the first suspicions
Of parting indifference; part in a play
Where signal promise is in the outcome for which
You have no care save for the thrill of a prayer;
Heaving in still air: Speeding on, stinging at the soar,
Spring at the air's roar; pleasures craze, all memory left behind.
Meanwhile do I stay to ponder the danger for me;
Eyes staring, unseeing with only regret and pain, disgruntled recalls
Of a past that is gone, staying, simply to disavow all knowledge of comfort-
Homecoming in safety to waiting stalls.

Poetic Prayer

If I should die, and yet remain
The object of this foolish claim
Of recognition of a life:
Of effort, interspersed with strife:
Confusion laced with wrongs and rights;
Poetic, selective blights,
Enslaved by dictates of who knows,
Of truth or where real knowledge goes.

Unchained melodies of rhyme,
Humming sweeter chords of time
That plentiful exuberance greets
This liberal excuse that meets
Each poor endeavour with a word,
Expressed in freer rhyme than verse,
And used in speaking every day;
Conjunctive verbal interplay.

And do you still express intent
At painful disillusionment:
That smile of real discovery;
Enlightened eyes in ecstasy?
That new sweet thing that stays the same
Through ages past and ages changed:
A human soul with human needs;
Emboldened flowering words and deeds.

Prayer

These books I read of dreams and sleep,
Dear memories in kindly keep,
All offer words of hopeful prayer;
Dear God! You must be really here!

Does kneeling make it more or less
Surreal to pray around a cross?
If someone knelt and prayed to me,
I'd tell them, "Have some dignity!"

Promise Man

You promised me!
Heart crossed,
Fingers crossed,
You promised me
And you lied!
Better tomorrows
Were the order of the day,
Disordered days:
Promised me I'd be better,
Better fed,
Better me,
Better led,
Better think again,
Promise man.
Politician!

Psychosis

Moods swing this way and that
With the vagrant dislocation
Of random imagery:
Fright-powered intensity
Foments anger
With an irrational dedication:
Rage bellows at memories
That feed these madness moments
With the devious sophistication
Of insidious villainy:
Question me in your wisdom
So that I might deny you:
I am church of my being
And your envy
Is my benediction.

Rainbow

I am nectar breath
Borne adrift on tides
That wanton earth scenes sway to,
Whispering at ages

I am mystery and smiles,
Blessing innocence with furtive glimpses
Of a truth and eloquence,
Liberated while I may
To shout my own name.

Remind me at your leisure
That you still want me
In your shared infancy,
Talking to me
With the excitement of your discoveries
And your bewilderment.

Know me
And call to me longingly,
That desire
Might still be manifest
In the opulence
Of your playful colour
And your renewed magnificence.

Rainbow

Glory, glory days,
And cloud and gloom are spent:
My heart and eyes are lifted
To the soaring firmament.

Your ray of arching beauty,
Your shining heraldry,
Reveals the constancy of life
In all its majesty.

My childhood days remember
All the stories I was told,
Of magic and of mystery
And hidden pots of gold.

You shining borealis
Born of joyful symmetry
Still means as much today as when
It served my infancy.

Raven

Share your gloating passion;
Whisper your secrecies
For my eager attention:
Cry loudly, leaden arbiter
Of mischief and discord,
Plying your eager path
Through these fields of prefabricated chaos,
Malevolence of grasping times:
You are the surreal parody
That is human strife
In all its magnificence:
How do I know you?
Misty recollection
Of all my bad dream residues;
Resurrected in your raucous cries
Of triumph and prayer?
Are you inquisitor or angel
To manifest my guilt
With your darkly foreboding presence
Of abject melancholy?
I feel your pain in my hunger,
And your answers are in the oppression
That abhors the very air
With a cloak that is your ominous mystery,
Home of a million dreadful secrets
And the end of the world.

Tree Life

Its time again,
Light life stirs aching limbs;
Feeding dulled senses
Like an unknotting waking child,
Warmed with a new vitality:
Sinuous pleasure messages
Instil the fabric of my being
With the joy of rebirth:
The bustle that is the waking,
Ripples through the folds of this mantle cloud
With a cyclic rhythm that is energetic survival;
Singing to me:
World things feed
And quarrel;
Part of me:
Tentacles, subterranean,
Meet and greet,
Drinking and feasting;
Gorging on my existence
And my prosperity:
Life clings to me,
Drifts on the wind and murmurs its stories
And its songs:
So do I live,
So do I shelter
And feed
And grow.
So am I.

Reflections

Transient as dreams
Are the mysteries of truths
That drift in and out
With the determination of a pain,
Disguised as friendship:
Light is aimless infamy,
Sometimes warm so that I smile in its comfort;
Sometimes devious,
Masking its shadows of intent
With foolish longing.
See me, be me, mirror me,
Tell me who I am!
You see me, I see,
When I see you:
Sad uncertainty,
Face to face with illusion:
Heart is home to frailties,
Cosseting trust like a spindrift,
Lest it blow away
With the emptiness of a spent dream,
Reflecting in disappointed eyes.

Reluctant Poet

Dear thoughts, how will you comfort me
And salve the burning in my soul?
How restlessly soliloquy
Seeks outlet on this hapless scroll.

A dream, encased within a sound;
The music of a missing word?
Vague tendrils feeding on the winds
Of timelessness, unseen, unheard.

Oh! Ageless vision, gently wrapped
In mystery and solitude:
The keeper of eternal flame;
The grain of rare ideas pursued.

Stillborn and sometime lost in fear
Of things unknown, yet meant to be:
Dear trepidation be my friend,
Lest I should live and die in thee.

Restitution

Alone, adrift,
Mired in the misery
Of a long dead promise
Of a time when fantasy was king
And love and kindness
Blessed existence
With the gift of personal happiness.

What follies lie
In that foolish optimism
Of misguided understanding,
When blind perception is ignored
For the passionate conviction
Of personal choice.

You have my heart and my soul,
But you mock them with your anger
And your rejection:
Your pain cuts with its severity
And the pleasure of your needs
Fills my heart with aching misery
And longing.

Yet still I dream,
For dreams are all I have
In my sad frustration;
Take my heart if you must
For your unconscious sadness:
You are my life and my restitution
And I have you every day,
In sad naivety.

Ripples

All I have to dwell on is a past;
Travesties that were first mistakes.
Errors compounded by errors
In the quickening course
Of this promising continuity;
Glaring like a gloating gargoyle
In an optimistic dream.
Still, I condone it all with a smile,
As if misery can be clouded
By the disguised acceptances
Of the undiluted lies
That constitute this existence:
I wouldn't really have minded rejection
If all that it had meant to me was a grin
And a charitable farewell
To all uncertainty and pain:
Belief that all I had to do
Was to turn a page
And start a new life
With a fond hello
And an even fonder farewell:
Foolish dreamer!
Scars ripen with tears,
Spreading their malignant fronds
Into every corner
Of hopeful expectation
This dismal little existence
Is ever likely to burden me with
In the name of ambition:
Pain that was impressed on me,
Usually by people who cared enough

To impose their own remedies
For the sake of their own Gods,
Knew that the short sharp shock of benediction
Never hurt anyone for more than a moment,
In their dilapidated scheme of things:
Sad memories that have dragged this pain through time
With an indelicate ease,
Into an awful eternity of repetition.

Roundabout

Round-a-round-a-roundabout,
Spinning, whizzing fast:
Clouds a-whirling overhead,
Faces flitting past.

Crazy, screaming, beg, implore,
Terrifying tears;
Fingers clinging on so tightly;
Laughing at their jeers.

Looks of gleeful malice;
Dervishes so wild
Feed the fear that dwells within
This wildly spinning child.

Frantic panic, faster still,
Hounding catty calls;
Sweating slipping hands let go;
On the ground she sprawls.

Sobbing uncontrollably
Mummy shares her pain
At the terror of it all!
"Oh, can't I go again?"

Seagull

Motionless arrogance
smiling at
Lilting suspension
Of tranquillity.
Flicker of rudder;
Of devil may care:
Swimming in atmosphere,
Floating in air.

That I was there with you,
Feathery friend,
Sniffing the air
Through your sensory veins:
Wafting on breezes
Of courteous state,
Easing and dipping
Your tremulous wake.

Laughing and singing
The song of the wind;
Drifting like chaff
In a sparkling hymn.
Soaring like sun's breathy
Heat of the day:
Bursting like cosmic dust;
Drifting away.

Second Coming

Your misconception about my role
In history's scheme of things
Might become clearer to you in the fullness of time:
You all continue to labour under the illusion
That I have absolved you from a lifetime of burdens
And given you unlimited access to an altogether rosier future:
Well! I want to tell you, right here and now
That may not necessarily be so!
First comings never quite achieved their promise
And the way that you lot have handled my love and care
Mean a second coming won't be too far behind either:
My blessings come to you at this feast of Christmas
But it would be nicer if word associations had been a sufficient reminder
Of the commemoration of this birthday,
Now that it has finally become a full-blown holiday:
The only thing abbreviated about it is the 'x'-word;
Who else celebrates with a name that is a kiss in shorthand?
An observation that is significant in itself, wouldn't you say?
And whoever agreed that it should be called merry?
We can all agree with the assertion
That role playing doesn't always bring its own reward:
You do your best of course;
Play by the rules;
Get betrayed by a friend and suffer a cruel death,
Hoping that it's all going to be enough;
Only to find that heroes are not that welcome anymore:
Still, a name that's revered as an expletive
Must involve some kind of recognition, positive or negative:
Sadly, it doesn't even merit a small thank-you
On the grand scale of mankind's undying gratitude's:
I enjoy a good Christmas as much as the next man

But the taste that it always leaves behind is the vaguely bitter one
Of an end-of-the-day feeling that if I had done things rather differently,
Perhaps the willingness of you all to enjoy it so blindly,
Finishing with "Auld Lang Syne"
Might still have made it the birthday celebration
It was originally intended to be, for M*e*.

Self-Expression

Infamy, or in for you,
In verses that might seem absurd:
A healthy hush is guaranteed,
Whenever these lines are seen or heard.

A need to talk and stupefy,
And hope that it will all make sense,
Are only simply understood
Expressions of my deference.

So frolic in your make-believe
And delve into a brighter day
With messages that cry for help,
Replacing infamy with play.

Selfie

Where's the rhyme and where's the reason.
Where's the sense in the absurd
Reflection of a simple lie,
And a softly chosen word?

Hidden slights and hidden needs,
Must-have moments in the day-
To-day inclusion of a lifetime
Spent in me-me interplay.

Look and see me if you want to,
Be like someone you perceive:
Plasticated poser person,
Trying harder to believe

In your briefest of narcissistic
Moments, can you really share
Yourself and all your picture secrets
Over here and over there?

Shadow Mine

Home comfort everlasting, ethereal alter ego,
Harbour of all failure and mischievous wrongdoing;
I grew so used to you that I could forget
You were here with me all the time.

Childhood mysteries were oblique distractions,
All-important symphonies of unreliable existence:
I even feared to step on you though I don't remember why:
Mobile photographic imagery; you were ever my companion in the
light.

You betrayed me in my games if you could;
Shadows wrestling with shadows:
I had to be careful to keep you hidden,
But we had fun together, didn't we?

Hand-made holographic images playing onto walls
Made you what I wanted you to be for a while,
But you always disappeared when the light came on:
You didn't really like the light very much, did you?

Did the dark mean that you could be one with me again;
Make me a slave to your own imaginings and your own dreams;
Symbolic terror places that cast me into the realms
Of a world that I feared to recognise?

So I'd seek you out in your corners and tremble at the possibility
That you might somehow become real:
I'd hide, cocooned within my bed, in the vain hope
That I might somehow be able to elude you.

Sixty-Nine

It's sixty-nine
And I feel fine
On alcohol
At any time.
I like to drive
And drink till late
Or earlier
For heaven's sake
Of joyousness
And devilry
May care
As long as you're
Still over there
Or over here
Or anywhere
where I can reach you
Any time
At speeds that keep you
In my mind
And in my eye
And everything
Is simply fine
In clothes that echo
Louder times
Of fallow fellows
Mellow yellow
Peace man
Speed man
Wham bam

Thank you, Sam
You played it just for me
That one last time
One last line
In sixty-nine.

Return to Snowdonia

I am glad of your majesty
And this confrontation:
Heart-shock hunger
Is a memory that seeks reconciliation
In another distant place
Or time:
Monstrous majesty,
Playing before these eyes
with your pall of humbling intimidation;
I rush towards the embrace
Of your batter truth;
The kiss of your anger;
The blast of your resentment;
Your need for a belief
That sad negligence
Was for a better purpose
Than the easy choice
Of an oh! So busy life:
So do I embrace you
As a lost lover,
Seeking the fruits of an absolution
That will live on in the petulance
Of your whole-hearted rejection:
I gasp at your lashes
And your spite,
Comfortable in the knowledge
That your anger will fade in the end
And I can bathe once more
In the warmth of your forgiveness.

Soliloquy for change

Sad ghost, you stay to haunt me with regret;
You misbegotten social dynasty:
Your timely message, all that was addressed,
Are angry tales that made us history.

Still nurtured are the dreams, when we engaged
In game and talk, on field and social stage,
And served our notice, tacitly declared,
That friendship be the mural of our age.

But truth and time have dulled these parting pains
Till none but fond reflective thought is left;
At least some comfort lives on in the grains
Of hopes and dreams we willingly bequest.

Sonnet for Adam

It's time to lay the secret of our deaths
To wide exposure and the light of day:
And innocence rewarded, painful breaths;
In present time will speed us on our way.

Mistaken sympathies that underline
The choices that we made when we began,
Still seem to have their roots in different times,
When fruit was rather scarcer than the sin.

Yet as each deed is newer than the last,
Experience with smiles still intervene:
Eradicates the follies of a past,
And then perpetuate an ancient dream.

And what if life were fair for you and me,
Would absolution serve this history?

Sorry

You're mad at me again!
Seems a way of life these days:
This thing,
You and me,
Me and me:
Don't ask me why it is that you hurt;
You do it so easily,
Basking in your insidious embrace
Of malignant energy:
Are we still friends?
Friendship so hurts;
Plays loyalty with truths
Like disparate chords
On the same instrument;
The same space:
I know your pain,
As cultivated as my own:
Sad searching
For reasons and solutions
That might permit our happiness
To continue to exist
In this anachronism
That is shared experience:
You have my regrets
With my love:
My heart and my eyes are yours
And our absolution
Is the mutual comprehension
Of our frailties and tensions
That foolish anger seeks to nurture
With unwanted memories.

Sound

We hear our sounds
And multiply them
All by several scores.
Might it not be better then
To subdivide the cause?
The feast of silence is the key
That does for us alight
Each sound as it was meant to be,
A prism of delight.

Queen at Southampton

Seagull and laughter songs
Compete in a glorious cadence:
Cacophony of careless appeal,
Irrelevant to this indifferent
And distracted child:
It arrives, but dully,
This droning messenger of the air,
Sweeping in with a grandiose elegance,
To alight upon the silvered Solent sheen,
Creaming oh so deftly
Onto this historic stream,
With ageless elegance and grace:
Who else pauses to savour
The image that is this aerial poetry:
Engines blare their defiance
As the water's anger screams its dismay;
Angry wake foams
In urgent desperation:
It bows a weather-beaten nose, carefully
To the subjective sea,
And coasts away,
Vanishing, finally, into the fold
Of its secret home:
Finally SHE appeared,
Distant, compelling
And oh! so beautiful, so brave;
Queen for a day:
I would always know when you were home;
Your red-black stacks dominating the harbour
And even the town itself:
You feed all of my boyhood memories

With your magic and your magnificence:
You glamour and wonder of your age:
How often have I visited you at your berth;
Watched you strain at your lines
Anxious to be on your way again:
How often have I coasted
Round your great girth,
Gazed up at your porthole-pitted lines,
Arching away into magnificence?
Black edifice of splendid majesty;
Your bow rising to an apparent infinity:
Alas now, I can only watch as you pass me by the shore,
Close to me once more:
Even the tugs, your helpers, your friends have deserted you now
As you display your full splendour
To my adoring view:
Unleashed, deceptive, free to flee
To some new world and liberty,
Your dignified symmetry,
Serene; sailing from my sight,
Till all that remains to remind me of your presence
Is a gentle rush of wavelets, gasping their desultory breath
On an unrelenting shore;
Your last farewell message to me.

Space Walk

I am dust life:
Cosmic energy,
Ethereal as breath.
Stars, dense as heaven light,
Form and fade,
Form and fade,
Tuned to suns day,
Moons night,
Sharing blinding radiance
And acrid darkness:
Relaxed, cocooned;
All is tranquillity now.
Surreal, inclusive,
Breath sounds beat on vacant ears,
Comforting this stark isolation with empty silences:
Together
We ghost silently through an emptiness;
Moon and man:
Earth world,
Blue, magnificent,
Rolling gently, gracefully,
Drifting with an easy elegance;
Portraying a crystalline majesty
For my delighted eyes.
The communicator interrupts the reverie;
One more working day.

Spaced Race

Dance like a fool
That reminisces with laughter
At the ruin of the world:
Space age dawns
On the need for personal space:
Person to person is fine,
Just so long as you're not in my face!
I'll drink with you and share your tales,
And laugh in agreement
For agreement's sake,
And all the while
The bar will fill a little more,
And spaces will grow still smaller;
I struggle to find a door:
Dance fool, in the space that you have
Where you all try to talk and all try to listen,
And everyone laughs
And tries to forget:
Tears dance in a murk of memory;
A glass half full
Or a glass half empty:
I can't even see the bar anymore:
I've lost my space
Race with humanity.

Spring

Wind breath dusts my cheek,
Wafting its messages
With the delicacy
Of a transcendental imperception:
Warmth bathes me
In a comfort of anticipation,
So that I bask in the caress
Of a brightly coloured, extended moment:
Clouds drift with languid affection,
Savouring the sky
With all its magnificence,
And life
For a while
Slows to an infinity,
So that I have to close my eyes
And smile.

Spring

Spring the sweet spring
Is a wish on a wing;
Is an essence of prayer;
Of a moment to share;
When the smile of the clouds,
And the blush of the day,
Are the gentlest of whispers,
Kissed kindly away.

Stansted Airport

Sad impressions curse the restless sleep-
Tossed dreams that broken promises waylay:
Are these the roars of wretchedness that keep
New hordes, in search of sanctuary, at bay.
Some expectations of a better rhyme,
Treat words like these as truth from high above,
Exactly as if that real word were mine:
Does truth equate to hope or push to shove?

Are bigger birds in need of bigger climes,
In lifestyles, grown without the sufferings,
Reliably reported and refined:
Post-dated and decided on the wings
Of all who live and need their day-to-day
Remembrances of pain to fly away,
To a better heaven?

(acrostic)

Stars and Gripes

Borne with pride, it billows out its message,
As untold worshippers shout out its name:
Carried high on mad waves elemental;
This passion of a joyful stadium.

Gloried as one for all their great achievements;
Symbols of oneness and new history:
Bellowed messaged voices, all uplifting,
Compose indifferences, too hard to feel.

Eyes, short on memory, in that one moment,
Trace flapping sheets of azured future dreams;
Dancing down below, those streaming champions
Bear rings of star-emblazoned stellar themes.

Embracing oneness in the world to come,
Brings starstruck hopefulness to everyone.

Suicide Note

Grey disgrace is melancholy destitution,
Weaving its web
Like a backward-running clock,
Seeking desperately for a purpose,
In one more vague memory.

Tears no longer give solace,
In this comfort
That is bland acceptance,
That 'attainable' isn't even a dream anymore.

Securities that were childhood promises,
Told by prayers and parents,
Fade into an insignificance
When confronted with the evidence
Of real disillusionment and deceit.

Dear death fondles with insidious whispers,
The ultimate lie,
That final release
Will bring its own smile of absolution,
And an end to the end.

Dear Louis

I'm a bit disappointed with Saha;
Still these times endorse greedy men,
Who rail at the name of their champions
Degenerate money and fame.

I don't mind the passion and mayhem,
The savagery need of us all,
To rage at explosive excesses,
In desperate need of a ball.

I might even watch them on telly,
That comfortably square brouhaha,
That passes for avid involvement,
And wisdom that comes from a jar.

But what do I do about sports men,
Who promise to fight tooth and tuck,
And die, if need be, providing the fee,
For playing arrives on a truck?

So yes, I'm upset with young Saha:
I know there's lots like him around,
Who'll stay for your shilling, if slightly unwilling,
Till someone else offers a pound!

TV

Light of my life
Bane of my life!
Would you be so attractive
If I didn't enjoy you so much?
Pleasing images make me resentful;
You dominate so completely:
Your caring comfort teases
With its devious mischiefs:
I could end you if I chose
Or whenever you choose,
But I do love to gaze
Longingly, as you,
Feeding me with your lies
And your misleading trickeries:
I might even fall for your beguiling colours,
When all I can do then, is smile.

Tempest

Mountainous rage,
Play your motion
As you play my fear
Sting me, venomous spray:
Dare me with your roar,
As you rant and scream your anger
And your engaging doom:
Steel to the rise,
Love the fury
Of your heaving majesty,
Towering and leaning ever closer
Towards that final nemesis:
How sweetly and brutally
I am lofted, so that now
I am lord of the world:
You Raging, heaving maelstrom;
Screaming pandemonium
Has become my penance;
An awful plummet into the abyss
Of restitution and admonition;
Nectar to a grinning seafarer:
Whitened knuckles scream their desperation;
Pleas are silent mouthing's
In the roar that is this beast:
A crushing embrace of arrival
And immersion so complete;
Swallowed, absorbed,
Becoming a translucent being:
Silence now
Save for the thrash of motion
And the pounding of ears.

Bless me once more with your love kiss, I pray you;
Sing your song for me a while longer
That I might still taste your salt-sore pain
In one more fear.

The Circle

Dark mischief, even day of mystery
And silence, deathly quiet infamy:
Vague shadows, formed of purpose sinister
Surround the fire with quiet nervous whispers.

The moon-pale glow of starkly shapen trees,
In awful witness, pray to be appeased,
While glow-light eyes in daring interplay,
Flee madly from the terrors of the glade.

Then rise ignited faces to the moon,
Of grizzled frame and dank foreboding gloom:
With cloaked countenance and ancient form,
As one exhale with rattling throaty groan.

"It's time!" Some eager gasp low's from within:
"Our master comes and bids us to begin."
Cold breath'd and spent the crouching crones draw near,
The warmer and more intent to appear.

As one, skeletal limbs reach to the sky;
"Oh, Lord!" they moan their coarse infernal cry!
"Today is hallows day and we await
Your judgement on our services and state.

"We taunt your true domain and spread discord;
Your children have and want and can't afford:
The churches, that are many disagree
And all bewail their sorry history."

What dreadful base of silence could afford
Some ancient longing or a cautious word;
Save fiery spitting crackling wood of green;
No sound but death betrayed that awful scene.

Then from the earth there came in wisped waves,
Gross misty sinewed vapours, deep decayed
Of odour, foul and cold, the rack of death,
To circle and take form and wickedness.

With dervish wail they circled round the flames;
Entreating all to join them in their games;
And gaping gaunt distorted faces smiled
Their willingness at this macabre divide.

With agonising step and stooping crawl
They gave grotesque promotion to the call
Of ghosted, form-like writhing waves obscene;
Deformed exertions in the evergreen.

And yet no pains could subjugate their joy;
These denizens were pleasured to employ
Their haste to speed e'en faster round the flames:
With glee they leapt and danced to dark refrains.

And now they cried their joy and heard it changed;
No longer to be stooped and groaned with age,
For blessed youth had vested, with a sigh
The gift of life on each forsaken child.

They ceased their mad exuberant melee;
Forsaking all, they screamed their liberty:
Then praised their Lord his gift of childhood sent
And in their pleasure knelt down to repent.

Still silence rested heavy with the pause
Though none dared look and face their Lord's applause,
But lay composed to sleep till dawn had come
When fire and crones and wretchedness were gone!

The Dentist

"This won't hurt a bit!"
Much bland assurance shields the beast
Of highlighted malevolence;
Poised loomed to take the feast!

Transposed, agape and well aware;
A frightful vulnerability:
I dare not move, rigid, affixed;
A prisoner in the dentist's chair!

Was this the succour that I seek,
The balm of pains that might have been?
Are digs and jabs I should not feel,
Sad penance for a past unclean?

such courage, such naivety,
I come and bare my soul to thee
And in my fright, you watch me die
And revel in your mastery.

So smile, but do not smile for me,
You subterfuge of sympathy,
For while my body cries in pain
My eyes and heart are closed to thee!

The King

I walked among the clouds
Until I came across a king,
Surrounded by his followers
Who whispered at the thing's
He pondered on as he looked down
Upon his world below.
He'd smile or frown as he flew past
While swaying to and fro'.

I walked across to meet him,
Upon his cushioned sky.
I wondered whether he could see
My house as he flew by.
The people all around him
Didn't like me being there,
But he just waved me come to him
And stand beside his chair.

He knew all that I wanted
And pointed at the ground
But it all looked the same to me
Upon his royal cloud.
The people all around us
Could only stand and stare
As though they didn't understand
Why I would even care.

The king just smiled but gently
At my bewilderment
Then waved his hands at all the world
Below his firmament.

"What you see below my child
Are those who share and fight.
But what I see is what I know
Of goodness and of strife."

I felt a little foolish
At such a silly task
As seeking out one little house
In such a scene so vast,
When all the worldly problems,
That happen all the time
Are happiness or misery,
To such a king as mine.

I'll wake up in the end I'm sure
And I sincerely hope
I'll still remember everything
Until I'm very old.

The Ploughman

The smell of effort drifts like nectar throughout the grime of one more
weary day.
Light, with its fading deception, plies aging shades of colour through
images
Where stillness still has the final word in this balmy evening play:
The signal phase of this reflective montage is the contented snuffle
Of beasts pausing in tired contemplation at the release of their ties,
And the occasional word of comfort.
Extending shadows reach out in searching skeins for places to rest and hide
With all the intrusive memories that only evenings with their diligence
can ever be privy to.
The plough lies now, in isolation, a discarded burden; sad companion
In its helplessness, for the birds that have pursued it throughout the day,
With a desperation of mindful experience:
Now perhaps they linger only because a farewell is due
and companionships are deeper and needier than the wastes that are words.
Shudders are the songs of chain and link as they sing of farewell
To the day and broadcast their liberation:
It's time to go home!

They're Off!

Shuttered, sheltered, shuffling in a line:
Spring-loaded, blaring snorting energy:
Uncounted eyes wait, eager for the blind
Explosion of full-throated savagery.

A single errant charger fights his goads
Before the gate, wide eyes disdaining all:
With calming soothing calls the beast is drawn,
Persuaded, pushed, cajoled into its stall.

They're all set now as expectation mounts.
Brave multicoloured riders waiting, all intent:
A crash, a burst, a cheering headlong pound;
Dictated power careers towards the fence.

Unbridled thundered, surging sweating hordes
Race neck and neck to screaming wild applause.

Thruppenny Bits

Ah! Dear old thruppenny bits!
Symbol of much that vanished forever
On decimalstruction day.
All the optimism of a brave new hell
Was dashed in those first utterances
Of that fateful morning:
"Sorry, guv! We don't take thruppenny bits anymore!
Two and a half pees is the least that I can do now
And that's the same as a tanner!
As for them half pees,
They're so small, aren't they?
I don't suppose I shall even be bothering with them
Before very long!"
I, on the other hand
Have always cared for thruppenny bits!
You always knew where you were
With thruppenny bits!
Solid and recognisable, like life always was:
I suppose change is best for all of us,
Only having to count up to ten
Cause that's all the rest of the world can count up to!
It's just a shame that when we used to count in bigger numbers
Things always seemed to go that much further:
Then again
As a nice politician once told me;
"Don't worry about your money, dear.
It'll still be the same!
Just remember,
None of this will ever affect the pound in your pocket!"

Time Being

Waken me dear child,
Ere chance should wash my soul
In a final memory,
And this poor state will leave
Only pains and recollections
Of past joys and sins.

Transcend regrets;
Mistaken harbour of this aching heart,
And let me see
Each instant of sad memory extolled;
Compressed in scenes as real
As liquid dream states,
Truth revealed.

For dreams are all
This dear existence, omnipresent,
Ever meant to me,
And timeless effort, seemingly eternal,
Blends its history
Into the substance of my total being,
Then fades from me.

Tobacco Road

Love taste never quite went away:
Love affair:
The hold;
The need;
The craving;
How do we all manage it?
Basking in the flavours of disposable discharge;
The smirk that is undisguised satisfaction:
I do envy them their pleasures;
God knows I've claimed them all for myself often enough.
Stopping and starting,
Always thinking that I could stop again,
Whenever I chose to
And then finding that I couldn't:
Only waiting for the right moment to come along,
When I might
Stop again,
Then start again:
It's all over now for good.
But in my heart of heart's, I still wish it wasn't!

Today

Attending change, these times are charmless misery,
All hawked as feisty lie's, a brand new age
Of expectation and regret, a time that seems too dear,
To be a true perspective to this sage.

Brave promises are sugar-coated fairy tales,
Of blessings that are served as daily life;
With smiles and salutations, easy time entails
Disposal of all trouble and all strife.

Hopelessly do I languish, with my sad regrets,
Consumed by an electrifying state
Of blissfully inert, remotely handheld sets,
That serve up all existence on a plate.

But will it hold a candle to a better time,
When living without comfort was my chief design.

Tollesbury Tides

Chimes that rattle in the rigging,
Call the early birds to prayer.
Stifled Latin chants, the sighing
Wind that hastens stormy air.

Guided home by expectations
Of the morning, of the song:
Stuka'd screams cavort and battle
Time, till timelessness has gone.

Interruptions, gently scudding,
Laziness befitting times:
Eloquence in rivulets;
Gently chasing rippled rhymes.

Proudly nonchalant he idles;
In his world and in his care;
In the comfort of a knowledge,
Generations know and share.

Salt marsh sailor, seemly silent,
In the bosom of the bay;
Calmer with the gentle swaying
On his prayerful holiday.

I could join you if you'd let me;
Sing with you a deeper song,
To the whisper of a breathless
Wading prayer to Tollesbury young.

Too Late

Regret still lives in memories compressed
At youthful hop, the local Mecca scene,
Where wanton time, restrained by awkwardness,
Meant foolish hesitations intervened.

With wild devotion, blatant bodies came and called
Their invitation notice to a crowd
Of seemingly disinterested boys,
Dispersed in groups, engaged in chatter loud.

If unity was strength, then did I sadly fail;
A need to be no different from the rest,
Foreswore the natural desire I had to win
The heart that called me out with eyed caress.

If folly lies in rueing thought, the most;
What price forsaken loves forsaken ghosts.

Trust

See a truth and share a lie;
Unburden your misery:
I could show you with a smile,
How easy pain unbared can be.
Should I tolerate your stories
In the twinkling of your eyes;
Dressed up in such vagaries,
Sincerity in disguise?
Truth and lies! Ah, what's the difference,
In the end and in the way,
That I love you with your mischief;
Dearest lover every day!

Twilight

Lapping wavelets chatter on the shore,
Exhausted by the effort of the day,
Fall and foam in idle rivulets
Of anxious times and carefree interplay.

The soft surf churns its gentle chorus foam
With lulling whispers, solitude and care,
And basks in moonlight, resting in farewells,
This slow, sea-calming stream of evening air.

The dying day is restless with its calm,
As seabirds search the brightly silvered shore,
In purposeful observance of their play,
They nod and dance their serious encore.

As even time serves subtle alchemies,
So night-time's cloak embraces mysteries.

Unemployment

Empty parking spaces,
Empty nervous faces,
Gloom pervades this scene of shattered dreams:
Thoughts so self-contained,
So secretive, restrained,
Speak volumes for this scene of might-have-beens.

All those brave new worlds,
All those dreams unfurled,
Lay dying for that mean unwelcome phrase:
Fearful thoughts condemn
These melancholy men
To insecurity and lonely days.

Save these lonely times
Of misery and crime,
When real employment lies in disarray:
And job security,
That final fallacy,
Is friendless arbiter of life's malaise.

Vocal Mirror

Vocal mirror, do I know you;
Vision of a stranger me?
Less than comfortable reminder
Of a self I never see:
Audio and visual
Mirror, imaginary,
Evidently makes the picture,
Safe familiarity.

Waking Dreams

Asleep, awake,
Sleep-wakes endless journey,
Through subliminal existences
And onward to nowhere.
Time, not here,
Not in this place where all is now
And now just seems to be,
Then disappear.
Yet there are times,
I see you as you are,
Beneath your veil of rational perception,
Of pure imagination,
In random flow,
And then who knows
Whether I'll choose to stay a while,
Or go!

Wall Art

Do I enjoy wall art?
All the best artists of prehistory did it
And it didn't hurt them too badly,
Or the causes that they all espoused;
Not too harmful at the end of the day!
Colours are better today,
Brighter, brasher, braver,
With perhaps a shade too much angst for my taste,
As well as being a little too short on storyline.

Do I enjoy wall art?
Symmetrical brick design, neat in its own way,
Doesn't really lend itself
To what I like to think of as imaginative stimuli:
Words that float in lurid sparks
Are lost in a blaze of vivid arrogance
To those that seek real understanding:
The right to deface,
Rather than the need to say anything
Of real importance!

Do I enjoy wall art?
Not as much as children do, it would seem;
Confused about what it says,
Rather than how it displays:
Walls need it like a tepid coat
Of careful introspection:
Maybe it's just as well
That wall art won't outlive the space that it fills:

Truth will be wherever I can find it
But having it bawled out at me
In lurid cacophonies
Means it will always lose its message
In the end.

War

Demon beast, plenipotential
Conscious travesty:
Seed ignominy still
We freely welcome thee:
Sad blindness yet, we draw our strength,
Insane hypocrisy!
Safe knowledge in our Mother Earth;
We live and die in thee.

Good plaudits and refrains we share
With those who won and lost:
The cries of half-brave heroes
Left alone to weigh the cost:
What peace was it that left them there,
To wonder at their sin?
Sad questions from the soul of man
For them to suffer in.

Dear children, in your joy and pain
Remember who it was,
Invoked the cry for peace
And said there had to be a cause:
Then ask them if the time has come
To find a better way
To shape the course humanity
Will take to judgement day.

War

Cruel deceiver, still you play
Your music for the soul of man:
Brave promises and sweetened pills
Embrace with lie and heady plan.

Excitement, celebrated cause
Will curse your true sincerity;
Your cruelty and wickedness,
Belligerent humanity.

So easily and willingly,
Will they all rally to the cry,
Till foolishness and ignorance
Leave them awaking as they die.

Water

Tell me in your own good time
About your purpose at life and death:
Wasting away on a tide of memories:
You squander your diluted nightmares
With the lies that have been your purity:
I seek these excuses for the sake of my stories,
And feed off you, become you:
Add your own small part
To my own sins, and the sanctity
Of my own surreal confusion:
Dance with me on winds of wonder
And make the world your own;
Carrying the inflection of your own pain
Into the four corners that you have made yours;
As you have loved and are loved,
In the name of life.

Why Not

Misshapen concepts plague the vast divide,
Between the great distributor of sins,
And all the good intentions cast aside,
That gave existence meaning to my dreams.

Still take my hand and lead me by my soul,
Through mischief minefields, scatter rugs of play,
For all the world as if the lie of gold
Was true perception, governing each day.

And if in pause I question what I do
To ease the painful legacy that age
With cultivated doubt, has misconstrued;
Will disappointment share this centre stage?

If love is lacked and love of life is killed;
Still, life is stilled when life is unfulfilled.

Wish

Wishful thinking, wish me well
That I might bathe in blossoms' bell:
So sweet that all the dreams I heed
Will please this sense and sense this plea.

I wish for all the world as if
My wish alone was lasting bliss,
And twilights of forgetfulness
Were morning's sensitive caress.

Oh! Star-borne messenger at play,
Your fiery message tends the day
With garnered, instant hopes and dreams
And swift displays of fiery beams.

Woodland Walk

Trees whisper their welcome
With mysterious songs of breathless silences;
Calming indifference to a dying day;
Fading with the ebbing light of one more play,
That begs me stay.

Shadowy rustles are the darker secrets
That warn of alien kindnesses;
Caresses of reassurance,
Dispelling forever all the terrors of a past childhood:
Daring my fears.

Dusky and deep, embrace this life
Of benevolent fellowship and a menial death:
Intrusive trepidation that lurks in the sultry shadows
Of a moon that bathes all of its own
In the restlessness of a crueller existence,
And leads me to home.

Words

Eyes!
Passing, meeting,
Fleeting, greeting,
Knowing!
Such brief instances
Of brilliant comprehension:
Such language;
Such completeness!

Oh! sad suspicion;
To doubt your true integrity
Is my innate deceit:
It gives me pause
To see what can't be hidden;
To be what really is!

Nakedness,
Shielded with words;
Lest a perception
Of my inner soul,
My secret being,
Be discovered, uncovered;
Laid bare before
These telepathic eyes!

Still seeking:
Hoping against hope
That looks
Will belie the inconsistency
Of my own doubts,

Nurturing a vague conviction
That all I ever needed to know
Is laid inside my bared soul,
And words are just confusion
After all!

Youth

I could have become what you wanted me to be
If I had held on to all the things
That you had told me were important.

I could even have presumed on my naivety
And smiled for your satisfaction,
And your soul.

How much did I want to be the person
That I thought you wanted me to be?
Does it still work for you?

Do you still see through the sham
That you yourself have been a party to,
For most of your own life?

In the accepted scheme of things,
I can only confirm my life in terms
That continue to register as failures.

Suffer me in silence,
As I dwell on the misery of that place,
And cry alone.

A Zealot's Prayer

Distance yourself from all shame
And all disgrace.
My death is in the well of tears,
Drowning in this ministry
Of intolerance:
Uneasy laughter regales my fears,
With the distraction of blame
And recrimination:
Nation speaks peace unto nation
With downcast desperation:
The laurel and the gun
Making for an uneasy alliance:
For more and for less
Will death be the prize
And the leveller of all promises:
I who have nothing,
Have nothing to give but myself.

%%%%%%%%%%%%%%%%%%%